IS GOD ON
AMERICA'S
SIDE?

IS GOD ON AMERICA'S SIDE?

THE SURPRISING ANSWER AND HOW IT AFFECTS OUR FUTURE

ERWIN W. LUTZER

MOODY PUBLISHERS
CHICAGO

Editor: Jim Vincent
Interior Design: Ragont Design
Cover Design: The DesignWorks Group, Inc.
Cover Image: Shutterstock #10969564

ISBN: 978-0-8024-8952-4

We hope you enjoy this book from Moody Publishers. Our goal is to provide high-quality, thought-provoking books and products that connect truth to your real needs and challenges. For more information on other books and products written and produced from a biblical perspective, go to www.moodypublishers.com or write to:

Moody Publishers
820 N. LaSalle Boulevard
Chicago, IL 60610

1 3 5 7 9 10 8 6 4 2

Printed in the United States of America

CONTENTS

ASKING THE QUESTION:

Is God on America's Side?

"I'M GOING TO SAY IT. In this war against terrorism, God is on our side. I know that God is good, and because God is good, we are good people. God is on our side."

Those are the words of a radio commentator following the 9/11 terrorist attacks. Although the 2001 attacks on the World Trade Center's Twin Towers in New York and the Pentagon in Washington, D.C., are now more than seven years old, the United States not only continues its war on terrorism, but many citizens continue to believe (or at least hope) God is indeed on our side. And with the election of a new president this year, many believe our new leader will have the assistance of a God who loves America, the land of hope and freedom of religion.

We can understand why it is popular to believe that "God is on our side." After all, many are quite convinced that since we were not as bad as "the other side" surely we Americans could depend on God to take up our cause in the war against our enemies. The radio commentator concluded in 2001 that a good God would assist the "good people" of the United States. So we must ask today: Can we count on God being on our side?

I became a United States citizen just a few years ago. I entered the United States as a Canadian citizen back in 1970, but finally I decided it was time to become a citizen of the country I had come to love. And so I write this book as an American, but more importantly as one who believes that the Bible has much to say about God's relationship to the nations of the world.

Why does the question of whether God is on our side deserve a careful answer?

First, we need to clearly see the role of God in our present political situation. In the recent past we have had evangelical ministers who have publicly endorsed one political candidate or another, thus implying that there was a right way for us as Christians to vote over against a wrong way for us to vote. Once again Christianity has become entangled in a partisan political process and the essence of the Gospel has been lost in the wider culture. The better we understand how God is involved in government, the more likely we will be kept from the folly of identifying one political party as Christian and the other not. Of course issues are important, but we must not confuse them with the message of the Gospel itself. More of that later.

Second, we have to again address the question, What is the role of the church in government? Unfortunately, many books written on this subject assume that the Christian community is able to change the culture through political muscle and electing the right people into office. The premise is that if Christians elevate the moral climate of our nation, more people will believe the Gospel, and God will be more likely to bless the United States. But we need to rethink the relative value of such moralism at a time when American society is in a moral and political freefall. Once we Christians bring ourselves more closely into line with God's agenda for America, we might be better prepared to address our political and spiritual crisis.

This book is written with the deep conviction that we should be involved in politics, but in such a way that the church always maintains its independence. We must never allow the impression that the cross is a political message but one of personal redemption in all its implications.

Third, we need to warn against a kind of "God is on our side" nationalism that makes the success of the church dependent on the favor of the state. We need to ask ourselves some hard questions about whether the church can be strong even if seemingly the "wrong" candidate is elected to office. Can we have a vibrant church even when our government turns hostile to the Christian worldview? Or are the fortunes of the church tied to our political influence in Washington? We must ask these questions because we need to accept the fact that we will not always have a president and a congress that honor our Christian heritage. Indeed, the time might come when we will have a presidential administration that is hostile to Christianity.

I join with all Christians who are praying for a national revival. Indeed, it might well be that without one, we shall continue to drift into the chaos of moral and spiritual nihilism. What we don't know is whether God will be pleased to send us a revival; but I must emphasize that we are not helpless until it comes. Whether God sends a revival or not, *there is work for us to do and we have the resources to do it.*

In the course of this book I will express my conviction that many among us have been diverted from the path God intends for us. A discussion of whether God is on our side will help us define one more time what we really should be about.

As this book develops, you will see that the answer to the question of whether God is on our side is more challenging than a simple yes or no. We will have to think clearly about these matters with "a Bible in one hand and a newspaper in the other," as the theologian Karl Barth once put it. Our times are complex and our answer to this question must be carefully considered so that we are neither given to giddy optimism about what we can accomplish nor sink into a paralyzing despair.

Join me on a journey as we navigate the terrain of biblical theology along with the ups and downs of our own political fortunes. Along the way we will find some timeless principles by which we can judge our present political challenges. And in the process we can learn how to make a difference in those matters that really count.

Seven biblical principles will appear in our study of the Scriptures—principles that will help us understand God's relationship to nations in general. Then we will learn how to apply those principles to America in particular. Finally, let us rethink our own response to what God is trying to tell us amid the confusing voices both within and outside the church.

THE FIRST PRINCIPLE

God can both bless and curse a nation.

"GOD BLESS AMERICA!" is enthusiastically sung by the vast majority of Americans. We all want "God" to bless America, but truth be told, all who sing this song do not agree on the meaning of the phrase. The word "God" in the song cries out for definition.

All of us know that in recent decades, God has been banished from the so-called "public square" in American life. He has been evicted from education, from law, and from the workplace. In some schools, children are not allowed to draw a picture of the Nativity at Christmastime. Indeed, only a couple years ago one judge told a high school valedictorian, "If you mention Jesus in your valedictory address, you will wish you had never been born."

But when the 9/11 terrorist attacks happened, "God bless America" signs were everywhere, even on marquees on porn shops. Everyone thought that surely God could be trusted to come to our side in this war against terror. What could be more obvious than the fact that we have stood for democracy, financial opportunity, and freedom? Think of the good America has done around the world! Of course God is on our side, and if He isn't, He *ought* to be!

The Banished God, Retrieved

So after 9/11, to borrow a phrase from R. C. Sproul, God was "allowed off the reservation" for a few months to fulfill His responsibility to bless us. But once our nation felt secure again, God was safely tucked away, church attendance declined, and the so-called wall of separation of church and state was built a notch higher. God is even less welcome now in the affairs of our public life than He was before 9/11. Recently, I read about a girl who was wearing a chastity bracelet signifying her intention to be a virgin until she marries, but it was banned from the school because it was deemed religious.

God is consistently banished from science, economics, history, education, and government. The role of religion, we are told, is to bless the soul, but not to interfere with our lifestyle or public policy. When I was in China in 1986, I asked a tour guide about freedom of religion. She replied, "Of course we have freedom of religion here in China; people can be as religious as they want to be *within their own minds!*" So it is; many here in America would agree that religion can coexist with government as long as our beliefs are strictly private, as long as they are confined to our minds.

Clearly, the God who was briefly allowed to reenter American public life was not the God of the Bible but the God of our civil religion. This God is described by Sproul as a certain kind of being. "He is a deity without sovereignty, a god without wrath, a judge without judgment, and a force without power."[1] Or, to say it differently, the God many people sang about was just "a bigger one of us."

Almost every State of the Union message delivered since 1984 has ended with the president declaring, "May God bless America."[2] This phrase should reflect a desire for God's guidance and approval, but often it sounds like a special incantation to provide hope for the future and to obtain any extra help we can. And even during the election season, the 2008 presidential candidates continued to call upon God to bless our country.

During the months following the 9/11 terrorist attacks, God was expected to put His approval on the American way of life without expecting us to repent of our sins. He was briefly allowed into our public life only to give us benefits, not to judge us for our sins. The God who was allowed off the reservation was a God who was only allowed to bless us—not a God who could possibly have anything to do with evil people flying planes into New York's Twin Towers.

But listen to these words of God through Moses, when speaking to the nation of Israel:

See, I am setting before you today a blessing and a curse—the blessing, if you obey the commandments of the Lord your God, which I command you today; and the curse, if you do not obey

13

the commandments of the Lord your God, but turn aside from the way that I am commanding you today, to go after other gods that you have not known." (Deuteronomy 11:26–28)

So there it is: God gave Israel a choice of either being blessed or being cursed. And although America does not have a covenant with God, the principle applies: God does not merely bless people and nations, He judges and curses them as well.

Clearly, these words from God were not spoken by the God of American civil religion. The God of Moses is not like a book on a shelf that can be taken down when needed and then put back when we grow tired of it. So, when many people say "God bless America," they mean various things. They may simply mean, "Lord, I pray that You will protect us; especially I pray that my family might not die," or "May I live in good health, may I be able to pay my mortgage, and above all, Lord, may the stock market not fall so my retirement is secure." They implore the God who does not call upon us to forsake our cultural idols but rather invites us to indulge ourselves. This is the God of the American flag. In contrast, the God of Moses and of the Old Testament Scriptures is the God who invites us to choose: "Choose Me and receive blessing; disobey Me and be cursed."

GOD ON A LEASH

Several years have passed since the 9/11 attacks—a time of tragedy when God was used like cleaning fluid to mop up the spill and, when finished, put back into the cupboard. Today He is told to stay put on the other side of the wall of separation of church and state. There He is expected to wait patiently until we have another tragedy—and then we'll carefully bring Him out on a leash so that He can bless us once more. To quote Sproul again, "We allow for God's providence as long as it is a blessing, but we have no room for God's providence if that providence represents some kind of judgment."[3]

But the God of the Bible does not limit Himself to blessing a nation.

Consider: Although the nation Israel was in covenant relationship with Yahweh and therefore could claim His blessing in ways that we cannot, even they were often severely judged. Twice God had other nations take His own covenant people from the land He gave them and had them transported to other nations as a judgment. The ten northern tribes were carried off to Assyria; the southern tribes of Judah and Simeon were taken to Babylon for seventy years, until almost all the older people died and only their children could return. All these judgments and others too numerous to count were brought on by God to judge His own covenant people!

Startling though it might seem, there are times when God actually is described as fighting against His own people, "But they rebelled and grieved his Holy Spirit; therefore he turned to be their enemy, and himself fought *against* them" (Isaiah 63:10, italics added). Imagine, God fighting against His own people! If Israel could not take His blessings for granted, neither can we.

If God so severely judged a nation that had a unique covenantal relationship with Him, think of how He might judge

America, a nation that cannot claim such a relationship. The God of the Bible will not endlessly tolerate idolatry and benign neglect. He graciously endures rejection and insults, but at some point, He might choose to bring a nation to its knees with severe discipline. As we shall see, sometimes those nations never recover.

ON GOD'S SIDE

1. Describe the wall of separation between church and state. In what ways does a view of God as "the God of our civil religion" fall short of the God of the Bible?

2. Discuss some ways God has been banished from science, economics, history, education, and government. What impact has His banishment from those disciplines had on our culture, our families, and even the church?

3. What does Deuteronomy 11:26 teach us? Can we expect God to bless our nation, even if we do not repent of our sins?

4. The Bible tells us that God judged His people, Israel, by allowing their enemies to take them into captivity. In America, what are some obvious cultural idols or examples of neglect of God that could bring His judgment?

THE SECOND PRINCIPLE

*God judges nations based on the amount
of light and opportunity they are given.*

AS YOU PROBABLY KNOW, the entire history of the Old Testament is the history of one nation, namely, Israel. Other nations enter the story only when they connect with Israel, either in battle or in the forming of alliances. And because of Israel's unique relationship with God, the nation is judged more strictly than its neighbors.

For example, consider how patient God was with the Canaanites, the people whom the Israelites would conquer. It took four hundred years before their "cup of iniquity" was full, and then judgment fell upon them when Joshua entered the land. God was similarly patient with Nineveh, particularly after her dramatic repentance as recorded in Jonah 3.

In the final analysis, God apportions judgment with the amount of spiritual light and truth given to any particular person or nation.

Paul pointed out that in the end time, God would individually judge Jews and Gentiles by the amount of light they had when they were alive. But the same principle, that responsibility is based on knowledge, is found throughout Scripture. Read Paul's words:

> For all who sinned without the law will also perish without the law, and all who have sinned under the law will be judged by the law. For it is not the hearers of the law who are righteous before God, but the doers of the law who will be justified.
>
> For when the Gentiles, who do not have the law, by nature do what the law requires, they are a law to themselves, even though they not have the law. They show that the work of the law is written on their hearts, while their conscience also bears witness, and their conflicting thoughts accuse or even excuse them. (Romans 2:12–15)

We must clarify several matters:

First, *responsibility is based on knowledge.* At the end of time, God will not judge all peoples with the same standard, because of varying degrees of opportunity and light. In Old Testament times, the Jews had the privilege of receiving direct instructions from God, and therefore they were judged more severely, both individually and as a nation. Indeed, Jesus reiterated the same principle when He said that those who knew God's will and didn't do it will be judged more severely. Then He continues, "But the one who did not know, and did what deserved a beating, will receive a light beating. Everyone to whom much was given, of him much will be required, and from him to whom they entrusted much, they will demand the more" (Luke 12:48). Again, responsibility is based on knowledge.

GREATER LIGHT, GREATER RESPONSIBILITY

This same principle of apportioned judgment is stated in the book of Hebrews. Because the revelation of God under the new covenant is so much greater, the penalty for neglecting grace is so much more severe. "For since the message declared by angels [the Old Testament law] proved to be reliable and every transgression or disobedience received a just retribution, how shall we escape if we neglect such a great salvation?" (Hebrews 2:2–3). Greater light means greater responsibility and a greater penalty for disobedience.

Now think of the United States. We have had more light than any nation of the past centuries. Although America never was a Christian nation in any strict sense of the term, we cannot deny its Christian influences. Go to Washington, D.C., and you'll notice almost every government building has a verse of Scripture carved prominently on the façade or entrance. So much of a Christian influence on government is undeniable.

Many of our universities were begun with the intention of training men for Christian ministry, beginning with no less than Harvard College, the oldest institution of higher learning in America.[1] History professor George M. Marsden chronicles how schools of higher education have largely abandoned their Christian roots, in his classic work *The Soul of the American University.*[2] In America, opportunities to hear the Gospel can be found everywhere. We have Christian television and Christian radio, and the Internet features Web sites that explain the Gospel. A Bible can be bought in any bookstore, in contrast to many other countries where the Scriptures are either banned or difficult to obtain. No other nation on earth can claim such blessings with perhaps the exception of the ancient nation of Israel that enjoyed a direct relationship with God through its kings and prophets. Surely, we cannot endlessly dismiss God and disregard His law without incurring judgment.

National judgments are, of course, only temporary, whereas the final judgment will be individual and eternal. Every one of us will be personally judged after we die. "It is appointed for man to die once, and after that comes judgment" (Hebrews 9:27). Even the judgment of the nations that Jesus referred to was individual and personal. It is really the judgment of the "Gentiles" (Matthew 25:31–36). This judgment separates the sheep (followers of Jesus) and the goats (unbelievers) and is the judgment of all who are alive at the time of Christ's glorious appearing. Then in the final judgment after death, the seemingly haphazard judgments of this life are rectified and in eternity all the scales will be meticulously balanced. All of us will be accountable for that we did with what we knew.

WHEN A NATION'S SINS ACCUMULATE

Second, *when we speak of God judging a nation, we often simply mean that the natural consequences of the sin of a nation accumulate and are intensified.*

All sin, as we shall learn, has both immediate and long-term consequences. In fact, we as Christians also are judged for sin, for "the soul who sins shall die" (Ezekiel 18:20). But sometimes God intensifies such regular judgments to get the attention of an entire nation. Then sometimes His blessing is removed and the nation is allowed to go its own way to reap the sad results. In the case of the nation Israel, there were times when it was even too late for the nation to repent (see Hosea 5:6).

Some nations appear to have fewer consequences for their sins than others. We must admit that those temporal judgments we see today are often, from our standpoint, inconsistent and unpredictable. Some nations seem to prosper despite their obvious sins; other nations are judged more severely. But in the eternal and final judgments, all the scales are meticulously balanced.

But—and this is important—God does judge nations in this life and when that happens all of the inhabitants are collectively affected. Whatever judgments God sends to the United States will affect us all. Indeed, we are already being judged in ways that will be explained in a moment. For believers such judgments are only temporary, but for the unconverted these national judgments begin now and have their culmination in eternity.

The God of the Bible will not endlessly tolerate benign neglect. He graciously can endure insults, but at some point, He brings the nation to a halt; and the discipline is severe.

I am reminded of the words of Thomas Jefferson, who by no stretch of the imagination was an evangelical Christian. In fact, with the help of a scissors, he produced his own version of the New Testament, cutting out all the miracles and all references to the divinity of Jesus. This was his attempt to separate the sublime moral teaching of Jesus from the other parts of the New Testament that he could not accept. He referred to his endeavor as "extracting diamonds from the dunghill." Yet, even this man had enough knowledge of God to assert, "I tremble when I think that God is just and His justice cannot sleep forever." Yes, you read that correctly: "I tremble when I think that God is just and His justice cannot sleep forever."

Our sins as a nation have been committed in the context of great opportunity and great light. Therefore it is entirely possible that the God who has already begun to judge us will continue to do so with even greater intensity and more widespread devastation. That God has not judged us more severely is doubtless much more a credit to His mercy than to our own goodness. We deserve whatever judgments that might lie along our path.

We are often told that 9/11 was a senseless tragedy. But if we believe that God is sovereign, then there are no senseless tragedies. It may not make sense to our limited minds, but we know God is purposeful and just. As such, He was both judging the wicked and bringing His own children to glory. To quote Sproul one more time, "On 9/11 Christians perished. On 9/11, impenitent unbelievers perished. The former were ushered into the presence of Christ. The latter were sent into outer darkness."[3] For Lisa Beamer, whose husband died in the United flight 93 crash into a Pennsylvania field, it was an opportunity to witness to her faith; she reminded millions that all of life is preparation for eternity.[4]

I might add that something else happened on 9/1—America asked herself some hard questions about evil and about God.

There were reasons for 9/11.

Keep reading.

ON GOD'S *SIDE*

1. Read Romans 2:12–15. What does this passage teach about our responsibility for the knowledge of truth revealed to us? Given our Christian heritage and its influence, to what degree will we be held accountable as a nation?

2. Why is the penalty for neglecting grace more severe than for neglecting the law? (See Hebrews 2:2–3.)

3. The principle described in this chapter applies not only to nations, but also to individuals. As you consider your family and your circle of friends, how seriously do they consider the truth of Hebrews 9:27? What message can we give others to bring them face-to-face with the reality of God's judgment?

4. God sometimes intensifies His judgments of nations. Given Old Testament history, for what purposes might God take this approach?

5. Do you believe God has been graciously tolerant of America's sins? Might we be due for His judgment? In what ways might God be judging us now as a nation?

THE THIRD PRINCIPLE

*God sometimes uses exceedingly evil
nations to judge those that are less evil.*

YES, YOU READ THE PRINCIPLE correctly: God
sometimes uses the most wicked nations to judge those who are
less wicked. That was a lesson Israel had to learn—again and
again. God takes the side of the wicked when He wants to use
them for His own purposes.

Think of Israel, the nation blessed with undeserved opportunities. Eventually the people supported unjust laws, they
turned to idolatry, and in general aggravated God with their at-
traction to pagan idols. Their corruption eventually extended to
acts of violence and oppression of the poor, and God rebuked
the nation for their selfish lifestyle. Not all the people were spiritually corrupt; there were some who still followed the Lord, but
their influence was marginalized. When God finally revealed
His plan to Isaiah, it was shocking in its implications: God
would use the doubly wicked Assyrians to judge Israel for its
neglect for Jehovah.

After reiterating the sins of Israel, God says, "Ah Assyria, the rod of my anger; the staff in their hands is my fury! Against a godless nation I send him, and against the people of my wrath I command him, to take spoil and seize plunder, and to tread them down like the mire of the streets" (Isaiah 10:5–6). God had had enough of Israel's sin.

GOD COMMISSIONS AN ATTACK ON ISRAEL

Two phrases in this verse can best be translated to say that God would use Assyria as "the rod of my anger" and "the club of my fury." Don't miss the fact that God *commissioned* Assyria to attack Israel. God does not back down from the explicit assertion that Assyria is acting under His direction; indeed God goes on to describe the crimes that these people will commit against Israel.

We might imagine that the bumper stickers on Israel's chariots read, "God bless Israel." But God said the days of blessing were over and the days of judgment would begin. So *God's answer to the evil in Israel is the greater evil of Assyria!*

Although Israel had a few righteous people and Assyria, so far as we know, had none, this fact did not prevent Israel from being judged by these heartless pagans. That ancient Assyria was far more evil than Israel had ever managed to be is beyond dispute. The nation was intentionally oppressive and delighted in cruelty. They had perfected the art of torture, skinning people alive without a hint of sympathy. And, true to His word, God

26

brought them down from the north and let them plunder the land He had given to Abraham, Isaac, and Jacob.

GOD ASTOUNDS A PROPHET

God's prophet Habakkuk wrestled with the same theological issue. He complained that God was silent in the midst of widespread idolatry and violence in the land of Judah. God replied that He was not silent; He was actually raising up the Chaldeans who would march through the land, plundering, killing, and stealing (Habakkuk 1:5–11). With that revelation, Habakkuk was astounded: The silence of God was one problem, but the fact that God would use a wicked nation against His own people seemed to shake the prophet's faith to the core. But with further revelation, his faith was actually strengthened and he concluded that he could rejoice in God no matter how much suffering lay along his path (read 3:16–19).

Contrast Jehovah's stand to the supposed attitude of the Canaanite gods. In those days each Canaanite tribe had its own god, whose idol was taken onto the battlefield. If the soldiers won the war, they gave their god credit; but if they lost, it was because their god was proven to be no match for the enemy's god. The Canaanites, indeed all the pagans surrounding Israel, never thought their god would turn to fight against them if they did evil. In fact, because their god was only an extension of themselves, their deity was always in full agreement with their behavior. They could always count on their god being on their side regardless of what they did.

Not so Yahweh. He was righteous and would deliberately orchestrate the defeat of His own people if they did not obey His commands. The people could never take for granted that "God was on their side" if they shut their eyes to the evils among them. When they took the ark into battle, God was angry precisely because His people were acting like the pagans, believing that they could manipulate God and count on Him to win their wars regardless of whether they were a holy people or not. *God was saying that He is more interested in the holiness of His people than their military victories.*

Yes, God uses wicked nations to judge "better" nations.

AMERICA *IS* A GREAT COUNTRY

Now let's think of America. How good are we? This is not the place to list all of the goodness that America has done throughout the world, but we must pause long enough to confidently say that we have done more good around the world than any other country. Is there any country on earth that has ever had the freedoms that we have here in the United States? We can still worship in freedom and the Word of God can still be proclaimed by Christian broadcasters on radio and television.

America has sent more missionaries to different parts of the earth to share the good news of the Gospel than any other country. Americans are a generous people—almost too generous. We helped win the war against Nazism, and after World War II was over, we gave Germany money to rebuild herself. Similarly, after the war we gave support to Japan, money to help her rebuild her devastated country. In the twenty-first century, we continue to give foreign aid to nations all over the earth for many great needs, including the fights against AIDS and malaria, and efforts to promote women's rights.

When people in other countries seek superior medical care, they come to the United States of America because we have the finest hospitals. Some of our scientists have discovered some of the grandest medical breakthroughs. Would you for a moment imagine a world without the United States of America? When there's a tsunami, it's America that sends the most aid. When there's an earthquake, America usually is the first country on the scene.

WE ARE PROUD AND SATISFIED

Yes, America is a great and wonderful country with a benevolent people, but the question is this: May God use a very wicked country to judge us? The answer is yes. After all, we are among the leaders of the world in the production of pornography, abortion, and the acceptance of same-sex marriages. We have been proud of our wealth and power and have acted as if we have ourselves to thank for our many blessings. Our congress now enacts legislation that isolates God from people's daily lives. The judicial system, especially the Supreme Court, renders judgments that, in effect, banish God everywhere from the public school to the public marketplace. Local school boards have insisted that atheistic evolution be taught rather than affirming belief in God the Creator. If Jesus is still spoken of with respect, it is only because He has been redefined to fit the pluralistic spirit of the times.

The sins of the world are found in our churches along with the sin of racism and the benign neglect of the poor. As God's people, we Christians have been preoccupied with our own peace and affluence and cared little about whether our neighbor knows the warmth of our heavenly Father's heart. We have turned our back on full-orbed biblical teaching in favor of positive suggestions on how our life can be better if we just included God. In many matters of life we have substituted the wisdom of man for the wisdom of God.

God may indeed judge us using another nation with different and oppressive policies. It may be a nation where women are oppressed in ways that are chilling. It may be use of a nation that disdains freedom of religion and actually kills its citizens if they convert to Christianity. God may use a nation that is so wicked that it straps bombs on terrorists who target women and children hoping to destroy and maim them. He may use a nation that commits horrific crimes without a hint of sympathy or remorse; indeed He may use nations that rejoice when innocent lives are blown away arbitrarily. He may use a nation that takes delight in flying planes into our buildings and killing thousands. Yes, if He were to use such a nation to judge us, it would be in keeping with God's ways and character.

God may use North Korea to judge us despite the nation's promises of peaceful coexistence. God may use the country of Iran to humble us, or the present war in Iraq. God frequently uses wicked nations to judge other nations for their indifference to His revealed will and purpose. Ancient Israel was overrun by cruel foreigners and we might suffer the same fate.

Yes, such judgments might seem unfair to us. But God is neither unfair or unjust. We must humbly acknowledge that He has the right to rule among the nations of the earth. And He has the right to judge both nations and individuals for their sins (Daniel 4:34–35). Thankfully, the other side of the coin is that He has graciously provided both forgiveness and blessing to those who turn to Him.

AMERICA IN THIRTY YEARS?

If we dare to predict what America might look like in the next thirty years, we can look at Western Europe. By any account, the major countries of Europe such as England, Germany, and France, for example, have, for the most part, not only abandoned Christianity but disdain their Christian past. Their cathedrals are largely empty and now are affectionately referred to as "The Tombs of God."

In all of these countries, and many others, militant Islam is on the rise. And if Islam should take over—and most historians say it is inevitable given the population demographics—the great freedoms of Europe will disappear, the Christian influence of compassion and religious tolerance will vanish, and in some countries the children of present-day Europe will be forced to convert to Islam. Sadly, there is no example in history of Christians being given equal rights when Islam rules a country; at best the Christians have been allowed to live if they pay heavy taxes; at worst, they are jailed or killed.

Unless there is a miracle in the offing that we cannot foresee, the children in at least some European countries one day will be worshiping a different God, namely, Allah. Meanwhile Europeans are making concessions to try to appease the radicals. I've read that crucifixes are being removed from hospitals so as not to offend Muslims and that public funds are being donated to build mosques. Having rejected the light of God, the nations of Europe well might be overtaken by cruel and heartless rulers and eventually will have to conform to the heavy hand of intolerance that is so despised by Europeans today.

In America, the official policy is that the so-called public square is to be entirely free of religion. But this vacuum will not be tolerated by Islam, a religion that encompasses the whole of life and law. Not surprisingly, in the interest of appeasement, schools in our country are being built with special prayer rooms for Muslims. In Chicago, a university chose not to renew an adjunct professor's contract after Muslim students objected to his support of Israel. The professor alleged that the school did not give him a fair hearing.[1] So much for free speech in our universities!

We cannot claim that "God is on our side" in the war against terrorism. He just might let our enemies defeat us because as a nation we continue to insult the living God. Yes, God sometimes uses wicked nations to judge those that are less wicked.

The Battle Hymn of the Republic, used by the Union army during the Civil War, is drawn from the Bible. We sing of the glory of the coming of the Lord; "He is trampling out the vintage where the grapes of wrath are stored" (see Revelation 14:17–19). These grapes are thrown into a great winepress of His judgment. This makes the terrorist attacks seem minor indeed. God was sending a message to us through 9/11.

How quickly we forget.

ON GOD'S SIDE

1. Read Isaiah 10:5–6. What motivated God to commission an evil nation to judge His people Israel? Are America's sins any less wicked than were Israel's?

2. Read Habakkuk 1:5–11. What about God's actions and character astounded the prophet Habakkuk? (See 1:12–17.) Even in the face of suffering, what was Habakkuk's conclusion in 3:16–19?

3. In what ways are we a great country? In what ways are we a proud country? In spite of our generosity, would it be in keeping with God's ways and character to use an evil or oppressive nation to judge us?

4. Given the state of national and world affairs, it is indeed sobering to consider the future. What do you believe America might look like thirty or forty years down the road? As a nation, what first steps do we need to take to reverse our course? What should be the church's role in all this?

5. Discuss the question, Is God "on our side" in the war
   against terrorism? Would God use a terrorist nation or
   organization to judge us?

THE FOURTH PRINCIPLE

When God judges a nation,
the righteous suffer with the wicked.

WHEN GOD BROUGHT the Babylonians against Judah to destroy the land and transport the people to Babylon, Daniel and his friends were forced to accompany them. This explains why Daniel's example of courage is so relevant to us; he is a model on how we can live in the "city of man" with complete loyalty to the "city of God" (to use Augustine's terminology). The point is that when God made the nation refugees because of their prolonged wickedness, the faithful were also uprooted and were called upon to survive in a pagan culture.

While living as refugees in a foreign land, God told them to seek the welfare of the city to which they had been brought; in other words they were supposed to do good where they were now planted. Just as Daniel was not exempt from the national calamity that befell his nation, whatever judgments God brings to America would affect even His most faithful people.

Of course, God's people are exempt from those judgments

where the wrath of God is directly unleashed. Lot and his immediate family were rescued from Sodom, and Paul, when speaking of the great tribulation, says that believers are not appointed unto wrath (1 Thessalonians 5:9). But these exceptions notwithstanding, the fact is that to varying degrees national judgments affect all who live in the same country or region.

A CURSED EARTH

There's no doubt that there were believers who died at the Twin Towers at New York's World Trade Center. I've already mentioned Lisa Beamer's loss. Her husband, Todd, is credited with preventing a hijacked jetliner from being flown into a Washington landmark. Yet in his heroics he died, as did all the passengers, many of whom were probably Christians. Those trying to stop an evil act all perished while wrestling to control the United Airlines jet that crashed in Shanksville, Pennsylvania.

Whether it is a terrible hurricane, such as Katrina that ravaged New Orleans, or a major earthquake that triggers a killer tsunami,[1] Christians die in natural disasters. These disasters are also judgments on this cursed earth, and when they happen they affect us all. We must caution, however, that such judgments in this life do not discriminate between the righteous and the wicked. We must also be careful not to say that the people of New Orleans are greater sinners than those who in Las Vegas simply because "sin city" was spared the destruction of a killer earthquake or hurricane. In one way or another we are all affected by the calamities that come our way. Those of us who live in the United States are all on the same boat; when it begins to sink we all feel the effects.

This knowledge, that national judgments do not separate the righteous from the wicked, will help us in understanding our role in the midst of our nation that already is under judgment. (For more evidence of our national judgment, see chapter 6.) How we live when various judgments come determines our role as a church in a nation that is rapidly turning its back on God. We also are to seek the welfare of the land in which we have been placed, even as the cruelty of paganism is on the rise. We are to be here as servants in a world that suffers under God's hand.

FAITH THAT MAKES A DIFFERENCE

At various times the American church has demonstrated its potential during suffering. It stepped in when disaster struck in the form of Hurricane Katrina. Long after the 2005 disaster, pastors in the Gulf states and beyond, continued to lead their congregations in helping the victims. One New Orleans pastor, John Gerhardt, says that Katrina opened people's hearts to their present needs but also made them look beyond today to tomorrow, and beyond tomorrow to eternity. The high winds and water, he says, not only broke levees but broke walls between churches—racially, economically, and geographically. Even today many are praying together and helping rebuild the city. The church, says Pastor Gerhardt, can do what the Red Cross and FEMA (Federal Emergency Management Agency) cannot.

Regardless of the kind of disaster/judgment that comes our

way, believers can enter into the grief of others, pray with those left behind, and befriend the hopeless. Gerhardt says he tells his congregation every Sunday that he not only wants God to "show up" but also to "show off"—that is, they want to see His glory in the midst of suffering and despair. Many have come to Christ through this tragedy.

We as a church are called to meet the needs of our nation no matter what form the judgment takes. The breakup of the family, poverty, homelessness—all of these are our opportunity to say that our faith makes a difference in this life and the life beyond. Recently a man described to me how he and other Christian men in his city have organized to help the local police by providing chaplains for those who are experiencing trauma. I think of ministries to those with disabilities, such as Joni and Friends. I think of ShareFest, an outreach of local churches into their communities, with Christians helping in cleanup, repairs, and assisting the elderly and poor. The program, now ten years old, follows a "simple idea of uniting together with other churches to demonstrate the love of Christ" to the community.[2] In a hundred different ways, we are to be servants to the hurting in our fallen world.

We serve in the world with the full awareness that we all need redemption. Left to ourselves, we are filled with suspicion, greed, and fear. We will take advantage of others to enrich ourselves; we will become obsessed with self-interest, caring little for the welfare of our neighbor. God always calls His church to live differently, and today when we've lost our credibility, this is more important than ever.

The Fourth Principle

Let us share in the suffering of our broken world as servants, called to give hope to all who seek it.

ON GOD'S SIDE

1. Discuss the concept of God allowing believers to suffer in the midst of a nation under judgment, as was the case of Daniel and his friends. How do we balance such occurrences with the teaching of 1 Thessalonians 5:9?

2. From the Bible, we learn that national judgments do not separate the righteous from the wicked. How does that help us understand the church's role in our nation, which already is under judgment or soon may be under judgment?

3. Since the fall of man, the earth has endured a curse. What kinds of judgments are attributed to a cursed earth? What are some examples of recent tragedies that fall into this category?

4. How can God use the faith of His people to make a difference in a sinful and suffering world? What is the church's role during such times of suffering? Discuss some of the ways you or your church has reached out to help victims of a natural disaster or other community loss.

39

5. Since believers are to seek the welfare of the city wherever God plants them (Jeremiah 29:7), what should we as a church be doing to bring hope to the inner cities of our nation? And what promise does God give us if we do this?

THE FIFTH PRINCIPLE

God's judgments take various forms.

"DO YOU THINK THAT someday God will judge America for its sins?" I'd heard the question many times, but this time it came from a friend who was thinking of running for political office. He was trying to peer into the future to see what might be on America's horizon.

I assured him that, yes, of course God will judge America for her sins; but there was no need to pry into the future. The judgments for our sins are already happening. When it comes to the consequences for our sins, the future has already begun! We usually think that God's judgment is most clearly seen in war, natural disasters, or terrorist attacks. But there is another form of judgment that is even more evident: It is simply the accumulated consequences of our sins.

What do these kinds of judgments look like?

THE DESTRUCTION OF OUR FAMILIES

We must realize that all sin has immediate consequences. Recall the words of Ezekiel, "The soul who sins shall die" (18:20). Adam and Eve experienced some immediate judgments because of their disobedience, but it is the long-term consequences that have boomeranged throughout these many centuries. When God judges a nation, these natural immediate judgments are intensified and we can see the consequences of our sin more clearly. For example, immorality, like all sin, has immediate consequences but it has future consequences as well. And when these accumulate, we can see the judgments on individuals but also upon a nation.

Nowhere is this more clearly seen than in the families of America. One judgment of a nation's ongoing sins is that the family structure fractures. Read this judgment Israel experienced because they turned from God to serve idols. Be warned that the description is gruesome.

> And you shall eat the fruit of your womb, the flesh of your sons and daughters, whom the Lord your God has given you, in the siege and in the distress with which your enemies shall distress you. The man who is the most tender and refined among you will begrudge food to his brother, to the wife he embraces, and to the last of the children whom he has left, so that he will not give to any of them any of the flesh of his children whom he is eating, because he has nothing else left, in the siege and in

the distress with which your enemy shall distress you in all your towns. (Deuteronomy 28:53–55)

From here the warnings continue in their severity and heart-breaking descriptions. The same description quoted above is then applied to the mother who also shall eat her offspring. The warning ends, "Your life shall hang in doubt before you. Night and day you shall be in dread and have no assurance of your life. In the morning you shall say, 'if only it were evening!' and at evening you shall say 'if only it were morning!' because of the dread that your heart shall feel, and the sights that your eyes shall see" (verses 66–67).

Both times when the Israelites were forced to leave their homes to go to a foreign land to serve their enemies, these warnings were fulfilled. Many homes were torn in two: in some cases a few family members were killed and the rest had to fend for themselves. At other times, some family members died during these long treks. Starvation and war devastated the population and the sorrow of the people was incomprehensible.

Of course, these prophecies are context specific: Israel was warned that she would be carried off to serve a pagan nation as a judgment for idolatry. When judgment came, the consequences were quick, following a war of attrition; for us consequences may be gradual, extending over time to families. But the predictions stand as an example of how the sins of parents can affect the next generation. Recall that in the Ten Commandments God warned: "I, the Lord your God, am a jealous God, punishing the children for the sin of the fathers to the third and fourth generation of those who hate me, but showing love to a thousand generations of those who love me and keep my commandments" (Exodus 20:5–6 NIV).

So although we aren't refugees eating our offspring, God is judging our families just the same. He is judging us for our immorality and divorce though the breakup of the family. Twenty million children live without a father in the home, and therefore cope with all of the devastating emotional and developmental consequences. Just moments ago I spoke with a friend who told me about a fifteen-year-old girl who gave birth to a child. This young woman was the product of a broken home; her parents divorced when she was very young. Now the cycle of immorality begun by her father continues. Future generations reap the consequences of disregarding the commandments of God.

Mothers are weeping for their children and children weeping for their fathers. God has said to America, "You have accepted divorce, you have accepted immorality, you have glamorized pornography, and raised a generation who spend their time watching MTV" and the seeds of His judgment are plain to see.

Incredibly, one in every one hundred adult Americans is now in prison—that makes 2.3 million adults behind bars. Michael Singletary, retired Hall of Fame linebacker for the Chicago Bears, gives his testimony in prisons. He says he asks the prisoners, "How many of you had a warm relationship with your father?" He recently reported that he is still waiting for the first hand to be raised. God's judgment of the sins of the fathers is being visited upon the children and the effects will be felt for future generations. This is precisely what God predicts in the last verse of the Old Testament, Malachi 4:6.

THE LOSS OF THE KNOWLEDGE OF GOD

The judgment for a nation's ongoing sins can be that other religions and ideologies pollute the knowledge of the true God and paganism thrives. Listen to this warning given to the Israelites, "The Lord will bring you and your king whom you set over you to a nation that neither you nor your fathers have known. *And there you shall serve other gods of wood and stone*" (Deuteronomy 28:36, 37, italics mine). The ten tribes that were exiled to Assyria in 722 BC were assimilated into the pagan culture and have never been heard from since. These ten tribes—often referred to as the lost ten tribes of Israel—never recovered the faith of their forefathers, nor returned to the religion of Abraham, Isaac, and Jacob. They were forced to blend in with their captors and lost their identity either as Jews or the people of God. The knowledge of Jehovah was lost to their descendants. Thus the consequences of their sin multiplied and indeed had repercussions for future generations.

Today in America the knowledge of the true God is being eclipsed by our so-called tolerant culture, which is viscerally intolerant of anyone who believes he or she has found some religious truth. The suggestion that Christianity is a revealed religion by which all others should be evaluated is scorned by many. Moves are underway to silence the church, even as the nation gives unlimited freedom to radical liberals, pornographers, and pro-gay advocates. Religion itself is relegated to a veritable cafeteria of ideas where people can choose beliefs that are "just right for them." We are told we can choose whatever religious belief we wish as long as our convictions do not interfere with our collective public values. And thanks to those ministers who have confused the message of the Gospel with the message of politics, we also have ourselves to thank that the Gospel is not penetrating the wider culture.

Before our eyes the Gospel is being both neglected by us as evangelicals and diluted in the eyes of the wider world. The only message that can keep us individually and collectively from judgment is being abandoned in favor of a pluralism that holds the irrational premise that "all religions are equally true." But if you think that all religions worship the same God, just ask the prophet Elijah whether he thought that the prophets of Baal worshiped Jehovah like he did!

God's judgment sometimes blots out the light of the Gospel entirely. Jesus warned the church at Ephesus that if it left its first love, its candlestick would be removed. There is no church in Ephesus today, and there has not been one there for centuries. In fact, thanks to Islam, it is sobering to realize that there are no viable Christian churches in any of the seven cities in Turkey mentioned in the book of Revelation. The death of any church is a cause for sadness and remorse. If it happened to them, can we be sure it will not happen to us?

Is America under judgment? I believe that the destruction of our families and the loss of the Gospel is God's judgment for our compromises and sins. And, as we shall see, we as Christians are surely partly to blame. By either ignoring the Gospel or by sending mixed signals to a confused world about what Christianity really is, we have planted the seeds of our own spiritual demise.

I'll explain in a moment.

ON GOD'S SIDE

1. As articulated in this chapter, the accumulated consequences of our sins are a form of judgment. What are some of the ways we see this form of judgment manifested in our American society?

2. Discuss the two kinds of consequences due to disobedience to God. Why do we tend to treat lightly or even dismiss the long-term consequences of our sin?

3. Read Deuteronomy 28:36–37. What long-term consequences did Israel suffer as a result of God's judgment for Israel's idol worship? Can we expect God to treat our nation's ongoing sins less severely?

4. Discuss the erosion of the family unit in America. What are some of the immediate consequences we are experiencing? What are some of the long-term consequences we can expect?

5. What immediate steps can we take to strengthen our own families?

THE SIXTH PRINCIPLE

*In judgment, God's target is often
His people, not just the pagans among them.*

YES, GOD JUDGES the wicked and, as we've learned, when that happens, the righteous suffer too. But sometimes the real purpose of present judgments has more to do with the righteous than the wicked, whose final judgment will be eternal retribution.

The apostle Peter leaves no doubt that God's priority just might be His own people. "For it is time for judgment to begin at the household of God; and if it begins with us, what will be the outcome for those who do not obey the gospel of God? And, 'If the righteous is scarcely saved, what will become of the ungodly and the sinner?'" (1 Peter 4:17–18). God's people are number one on His list for both His care and His discipline.

We might be the cause of our own weakness as a church. In the story of Jonah we read, "The Lord hurled a great wind upon the sea," and the wind churned the water and Jonah was in a storm with these sailors. These pagan sailors were crying out to their pagan gods, and Jonah had the honesty to say, "This storm is my fault; it is happening because I am running from God." He acknowledged that he was a worshiper of the true God—of the land and of the sea, the one who creates storms and stops them. So he convinced the sailors that if he were thrown into the sea, the wind would cease. They let go of their cargo first, but then took God's prophet up on his challenge. They threw him overboard and immediately there was a calm.

It was a disobedient prophet who caused this storm. It is easy for us as evangelicals to blame the liberals—the abortionists, the homosexuals, and the American Civil Liberties Union for our nation's woes. But perhaps the responsibility for our country's turbulence has to be laid at the doorstep of the church. We who are running from our responsibilities might be the reason why we are losing the wider culture to relativism and nihilism.

WARNINGS TO CHURCHES

If judgment begins at the house of God, is the church today under judgment? Before I answer that question, I must emphasize that all who put their trust in Christ will not experience final judgment, for Jesus promised that those who believe on Him "shall not come into judgment, but has passed from death into life" (John 5:24 NKJV). But there is no doubt that in this life God disciplines His people individually and collectively as a church.

Recall the stinging rebuke Jesus gave to a few of the

churches of Revelation. To those in Pergamum who tolerated the "Nicolaitans" (those who justified immorality), He warned, "Repent therefore! Otherwise, I will soon come to you and will fight against them with the sword of my mouth" (Revelation 2:16 NIV). Imagine, Jesus coming with a sword to fight against the disobedient people in His church! To those in Thyatira who tolerated "Jezebel," He said, "So I will cast her on a bed of suffering, and I will make those who commit adultery with her suffer intensely, unless they repent of her ways. I will strike her children dead. Then all the churches will know that I am he who searches hearts and minds, and I will repay each of you according to your deeds" (2:22–23 NIV).

And to Laodicea He warned, "So, because you are lukewarm—neither hot nor cold—I am about to spit you out of my mouth" (Revelation 3:16 NIV). Clearly, Jesus never tolerates sin in the life of a church!

THE CHURCH'S DIMINISHED INFLUENCE

Might Jesus be rebuking and disciplining us as He did the churches of Revelation? I think there is reason to believe that we as members of the evangelical church are experiencing judgment. One sign of this is that *the church has increased visibility but diminishing influence.* The so-called Religious Right had great plans to reverse the moral trends of our nation. We are told that we have helped elect presidents and have impacted public policy and even the selection of judges. But by identifying these gains as those won by the "Religious Right," namely, Christians who are in cahoots with a particular party, we have made this nation believe that the church is a political base rather than the dispenser of the Gospel. Any gains we have made (mixed at best) came about at the price of the loss of the Gospel in the wider culture. We have cheapened Christ before a watching world.

Unfortunately, Christianity, in the minds of millions of Americans, is right-wing politics. I believe we are under judgment because we have cast about for a solution to our nation's problems and thought that it lay with political muscle and even with a specific political party. By becoming publicly partisan and implying that one party is more "Christian," we have clouded the issues of what Christianity really is. Religion is being redefined as politics; the flag has replaced the cross. And we are feeling the negative repercussions.

Today evangelicals are in the news not because of the Gospel but because of their political support or endorsements. The scenario of various religious leaders endorsing one political candidate or another is truly deserving of tears. Some Christian leaders have formed coalitions to "take America back." They want to "put God back" into our political, legal, and educational institutions. If they have enough numbers and voting power, they think that the hands of the clock can be reversed. They long for a return to a basic civil religion where everyone marches in line with minimal religious convictions. In identifying ourselves with a political party and battling for civil religion, we have lost our identification with Jesus Christ.

What Is "Civil Religion"?

Let me clarify the meaning of civil religion. Henry Steele Commager, one of America's leading historians, argued that "the new nation began with two religions, one secular and one spiritual. Almost all Americans acknowledge themselves as Christians" but in fact, "they generally shared what has been called a civil religion . . . a secular faith in America herself, in democracy, equality and freedom which were equated with America in the American mission and the American destiny."[1]

"The substance of such a civil religion," writes Michael Horton, is its "tendency to push God to the outer fringes so that He can be called on for state functions, but not get involved in the day to day thinking or operation of normal life."[2] As Tom Sine points out, surely we should realize that "time-honored civil religion and Christianity are two very different faiths." Indeed, he continues, these two "bow the knee to two very different deities and work for two very different agendas."[3]

But can't we serve Christianity and our cultural civil religion? Yes, but only if we understand the difference and not confuse the two. Unfortunately, I don't think we've always done that.

An example of civil religion is the recent so-called Christmas wars. If we insist that store clerks must say "Merry Christmas" rather than "Happy Holiday," what have we really gained? Are the people who are asked to acknowledge the Christmas holiday any closer to faith in Christ or are they simply irritated that they have to conform to our beliefs? And even if we win legislation mandating that the Ten Commandments be displayed in courthouses and classrooms, are we thereby bringing our culture closer to faith in Christ, or antagonizing everyone around us?

Certainly I believe we should keep the phrase "Under God" in the pledge of allegiance, but if it were removed, would the church be weaker? Christ and Caesar have always been in conflict, but I think it is time to affirm that *Christ can do well with or without Caesar's cooperation.*

For a time I was regularly receiving mail that kept me up-to-date on what products or services I should be boycotting. Whether it is against Ford, Disney, or Procter & Gamble, some people think we should let our protests be heard via our pocketbook. I've never been convinced of the long-term value of such a response. I found it hard to keep up-to-date on when a boycott began and when it was over.

We must remember that when these organizations we boycott promote homosexuality, pornography, etc., they are acting unbiblically: Unrepentant human nature will always pursue wealth, pleasure, and power no matter the moral cost. But if there are those among us called to protest these products or services, let them do it without the banner of Christianity, lest once again we are known for what we are against rather than what we are for. Whenever possible we must use persuasion for our point of view rather than attack-dog political confrontation.

We want a civil religion because we fear that we might lose our creature comforts if our nation is in decline. I fear that one reason why we are so anxious that the economy remain strong is not so much because we want to use our funds to support the spread of the Gospel, but because we all enjoy the American way of life. And we believe that a strong America always translates into a strong church. Perhaps yes, but then again, perhaps no.

We can be easily wrought up about corruption in government, the wasting of our taxes, the national debt, and funding of the arts. Often we become angry not because Christ is daily dishonored and the true God not worshiped but because we are fearful that our taxes and family values are not being protected. Some Christians can get more excited about what commentator Rush Limbaugh has to say than about what their pastor preached in church.

To put it clearly: For some Christians, lower taxes, a strong national defense, and lobbying to "keep Christ in Christmas" are more pressing issues than whether their neighbors and friends will spend eternity with God or be lost forever. Our defense of civil religion and our partisan politics are in the news, but our good deeds and the Gospel we represent are not.

I'm convinced that many Christians who are angry today would be pacified if only we could return this country to the 1950s when there were no drugs, pornography was sold on the black market, and movies, for the most part, portrayed family values. They would be satisfied with this change even if no one were converted to Christ in the process! They would be content if Christ were accepted as lawgiver to restore order to society, even if He were not accepted as Savior to *rescue* society.

Nearly all of us—myself included—love the American way of life; at Christmastime we want our living rooms to look as if there was an explosion in a department store. Yes, extravagance is the American way. But is it the distinctively Christian way? Many years ago, just before Christmas, I visited the country of Belarus, which had just gained independence from communist control. I asked my friend Victor Krutko what the stores carried for the holidays. He looked at me with a wry smile and said, "There is no Christmas shopping; the Christians just sing hymns, but there are no presents, the stores are empty, and the people have no money." Are they less Christian than the rest of us? I think not.

WITHDRAW FROM POLITICS?

If you think that I am saying we should withdraw from politics, you have misunderstood me. We dare not privatize our faith but apply it to all aspects of life, including politics. Christians have both the privilege and duty to vote, and if none of the candidates is to our liking, we vote for the "best" one. Above all, we have both the responsibility and privilege of praying for those who are in office, whether our leaders are according to our liking or not. Paul urged prayer for kings and those in authority— even when the notorious Nero was in power (1 Timothy 2:1–5)!

Christians should run for public office. We can as individuals join coalitions that lobby for those policies that are in keeping with our values, but we do not draw lines in the sand making it sound as if it is the Christians versus the world. The question is not whether we should be involved in politics; the question is what that involvement should look like.

Dangers We Must Avoid

There are dangers that we must avoid. Recently, an excellent document has been released titled "An Evangelical Manifesto," written to reclaim the word *evangelical* from the many misunderstandings of it in contemporary culture. This document properly repudiates two equal but opposite errors into which the church has fallen. One error has been to privatize faith, applying it to the personal realm only, thus our faith becomes "privately engaging and publicly irrelevant." The other error the document exposes is to politicize faith, using it to express political points of view that have often lost touch with biblical truth.

Regarding this error of politicizing faith, the document says, "[When] faith loses its independence, the church becomes 'the regime at prayer,' Christians become 'useful idiots' for one political party or another, and the Christian faith becomes an ideology in its purist form. Christian beliefs are used as weapons for political interests."[4]

Yes, by politicizing faith we have become "useful idiots" for one political party or another. Witness high-profile evangelicals endorsing political candidates, and lesser-known leaders following suit. No wonder a national news story on what Christianity is made only scant reference to Christ but concentrated on political power and endorsements. As I recall, apart from one reference, Jesus was nowhere to be seen

Read carefully this declaration from "The Manifesto," which aims to correct such misperceptions.

Called to an allegiance higher than party, ideology, and nationality, we Evangelicals see it our duty to engage with politics, but our equal duty never to be completely equated with any party, partisan ideology, economic system or nationality. . . . The politicalization of faith is never a sign of strength but of weakness. The saying is wise, "The first thing to say about politics is that politics is not the first thing." The Evangelical soul is not for sale. It has already been bought at an infinite price.[5]

The evangelical soul is not for sale! And yet, to our detriment, we have willingly identified ourselves with political candidates and their partisan rhetoric. We've become "useful idiots" indeed. As a result, we are suffering a backlash and losing whatever political gains we thought we would have. We should have known that politics is a game of high risk. If we live by the ballot box, we must die by the ballot box.

No wonder Ed Dobson, a former board member of the Moral Majority, changed his mind about the power of politics. He writes, "Politics cannot offer permanent solutions because it is based on a flawed view of sin and society. One of its premises is that if you elect the 'right' representatives who will pass the right legislation you will have the 'right' society. But we know this is not true."[6] We have forgotten that the reason the world will never share our values is because they do not share our Christ.

ENGAGING THE CULTURE WITH REASON AND GRACE

Yes, we should be speaking out on issues of justice and compassion. Christians have been on the forefront of legislation to pass child labor laws and abolish slavery, just as we should be on the forefront of speaking up for the unborn and keeping our nation from legalizing same-sex marriages. Let us appeal to reason and justice in our discussion of these issues, but whenever possible, let us not by our rhetoric force even moderate people to turn against us.

When we engage the culture on important issues, thanks to what theologians call common grace, we might find that many people who are not specifically Christian will support us. This is, in my opinion, the proper use of what Francis Schaeffer used to call "cobelligerency." But let us not politicize these issues and unwittingly give the impression that these agendas are the sum of the Christian message. We must always distinguish between the essence of Christianity, namely, God's redemptive work in Christ, and its social and moral effects.

We should especially guard against having a church or minister endorse a political candidate. We should jealously reserve the word *Christian* for the core of what we believe, namely, the Gospel of Jesus lived out through acts of compassion. Yes, we should do all we can to influence policy but we do so maintaining the independence of the church from political labels and entanglements. I grieve because for many observers *the cross of Christ appears as a dilapidated bulletin board cluttered with a whole host of issues!*

Ask any average American what Christians believe and he will give you multiple answers, some correct, but most misleading. Almost all will say that Christianity is a conservative political viewpoint that wants to "impose" its morals on others. We might protest that the criticism is unfair, but the fact remains that we have ourselves to blame for the confusion. Few will say that the central doctrine of Christianity is that Christ came into the world to save sinners. If we are in the news, let it not be because of whom we support politically, but because of our ability to speak to the issues and because of the way we live and because of whom we worship.

Many of us know that fundamentalists/evangelicals have always been critical of the theological liberals who ceased preaching the Gospel in favor of political and social action. Incredibly, the same charge can now be laid at the feet of the evangelical community, with its emphasis on political muscle, boycotts, and the desire to "have a place at the table" with our political leaders. The concerns are different, but the methods are the same. Yes, I believe we are under judgment because we have sought political power more fervently than we have sought personal holiness coupled with our collective and individual witness to the power of the Gospel. Chesterton was right: a coziness between church and state is good for the state but bad for the church.

Which leads to my next point.

A LACK OF SPIRITUAL POWER IN OUR CHURCHES

Second, I believe we are under judgment because our churches have become spiritually anemic. We have much preaching and teaching coupled with the latest technology, but we cannot point to many changed lives. "Our church," one man told me, "has a budget of five million dollars, but we haven't had anyone saved in years." And, in order to make up for our spiritual powerlessness, we have substituted sermons and seminars filled with therapeutic advice on how we can live better lives if we just took advantage of new insights about human relationships and steps to success.

Worse, *we appear to have become ashamed of the Gospel.* A Muslim family in Texas recently converted to Christ at great personal cost. They attended a large church with the hope that they would hear a word that would give them encouragement and hope. Instead the pastor—evidently an evangelical—preached a sermon on the benefits of good nutrition. I wish I could say that this is an isolated and extreme example, but the fact is that the Gospel has taken second place in many churches. Even those who believe the Gospel have substituted the distortions of health and wealth, and the trappings of a feel-good religion. No wonder many Christians are intimidated by the culture and make virtually no attempt to share the Gospel with their friends and coworkers.

Incredibly, for the most part the church has abandoned the very message that is most desperately needed at this critical hour of history. At a time when we need to engage our culture with the one message that has any hope of transforming it, many among us have turned aside to fight the world on its own terms and with its own strategies. The temptation of the church has always been to confuse the kingdom of this world and the kingdom of God and we are reaping the results.

TIME TO RECALL THE POWER OF THE CROSS

At times committed Christians seem to have forgotten that God's power is more clearly seen in the message of the cross than in any political or social plan they might devise. Might not our search for some antidotes to our grievous ills be symptomatic of our lost confidence in the power of the Gospel to change people from the inside out? Does not our reticence to share the Gospel betray our misplaced priorities?

Recently I had lunch with a graduate of one of America's prestigious universities. He said that many evangelical students abandon their faith in university, not because the arguments against Christianity are persuasive but because of the intense social pressure of the students and faculty. The Gospel message, he said, is considered so outdated, so countercultural, and so antithetical to an accommodating, politically correct American society that students choose to either hide their convictions or abandon them altogether.

Whatever happened to the day when suffering for Christ was considered a badge of high honor? The Bible warns us that we should not be ashamed of the Gospel, precisely because it is so foolish to the unbelieving heart. But only when its "foolishness" remains intact is it "the power of God unto salvation." No wonder the church is weakened when we substitute other, more "practical" agendas.

As a consequence, we should not be surprised that our behavior mirrors that of the world. Jesus taught that the church is to be in the world as a ship is in the ocean, but when the ocean gets into the ship, the ship is in trouble. Morally and spiritually we are taking on water. By buying into the world's values and pleasures, we have diluted our impact and we are suffering for it. Opinion polls regularly show the similarity between the behavior of evangelicals and the world, so our spiritual need is obvious.

The Jesus of the book of Revelation is observing, rebuking, and wooing us all at the same time. We desperately need to return to our first love, and return to the passionate teaching and preaching of God's Word, lived out in His people. Yes, judgment begins at the house of God, and I think it has begun.

The Christian influence in America is eroding daily. The opinion polls show that most Americans believe in God, but many live as practical atheists, paying little attention to the Bible as God's revelation. The proliferation of New Age thought, the radical individualism that clamors for personal rights, and the privatization of morality tears at the very fabric of our families and institutions. Humanism is now coming to its logical conclusions in education, law, and morality. The result is as bad as the Founding Fathers imagined it might be.

It is time for us to take up the cross of our Savior and carry it triumphantly into the world.

ON GOD'S *SIDE*

1. Read 1 Peter 4:17–18. What is the apostle Peter's point? For what purpose does God discipline His own people? A key cross reference to consult is Hebrews 12:5–6.

2. Discuss the suggestion that the responsibility for the country's turbulence be laid at the doorstep of the church. Can you identify where the church has failed to hold its ground against society's philosophies?

3. What is the first sign that the church is under judgment? What price has the church paid for its increased visibility, for example, in the political arena?

4. As emphasized in the document "An Evangelical Manifesto," the church has fallen into two equal but opposite errors. List the two errors and describe the consequences that result from both errors.

5. Has the church of Christ become ashamed of the Gospel? What challenges do we face today in sharing our faith with others? As an encouragement for others in your group, relate experiences you have had sharing your faith.

THE SEVENTH PRINCIPLE

God sometimes reverses intended judgments.

GOD'S BLESSING ON ANY NATION is undeserved. When God blesses America, it is not because we have earned it for good behavior. Sometimes God simply blesses a nation for reasons that are not known to us, intending that His goodness should lead us to repentance. At other times He responds to the desperate desire of His people to bring their lives in line with His will and purpose. Think of a few of the instances where God granted unexpected mercies.

Read the Old Testament and sometimes you get the impression that Israel regularly ignored the extended messages of the prophets. Almost all of them were preaching "doom and gloom," but for the most part, the people didn't have the heart to care. But on several occasions they did respond, and judgment was averted.

Sometimes we have to unpack the chronology of the Old Testament to understand a book in its setting. Take the prophet

Micah, for example. Although his book occurs later in the Old Testament writings, Micah actually preached a hundred years *before* Jeremiah. Micah warned Judah that her "wound is incurable" and that oppressors were on their way to overrun the land. Nowhere in the book is there much reason to believe that anyone was listening. He probably thought he was just spitting into the wind.

Incredibly, a century later, Jeremiah is being brought before the priests and false prophets of the land who want to see him killed. After hearing the case, the officials conclude that they will not put Jeremiah to death and they appeal to the preaching of Micah, and ask two questions: "Did Hezekiah king of Judah and all Judah put him to death? Did he not fear the Lord and entreat the favor of the Lord, and *did not the Lord relent of the disaster that he had pronounced against them?*" (26:19, italics added). The point is that Hezekiah listened to Micah's words and sought God who withheld coming judgment. Yes, the preaching of a discouraged prophet caused the king to entreat the favor of God and the predicted disaster did not come to pass.

We think of God's grace to Nineveh, that evil city that responded immediately to the preaching of Jonah. The prophet's message was clear, "Yet forty days and Nineveh shall be overthrown." But implied in the warning was the condition that if they repented, God would relent from what He intended to do to them. God sometimes has been known to reverse the judgments predicted when there has been repentance and faith. As far as we know, there is no inviolable law that says that once a nation begins its spiritual decline it can never reverse course.

Eighteenth-century England was in such a state of decline that Parliament had to be dismissed in the middle of the day because too many of the members were in a drunken stupor. Children were abandoned to die and immorality was rampant. The knowledge of God had all but faded from view. Mercifully, God reversed that trend through the preaching of John Wesley and George Whitefield. Some historians believe that it was the revival that kept England from the fate of a bloody revolution, such as was experienced by France.

Many of us are praying for revival, but if God does not send a national awakening, all is not lost. If we have faithful churches, preaching the Gospel and having a credible witness in their locality, we have the resources to halt our present downward spiral. Our problem is not that a national revival has not come; our problem is that we have not used the resources of God's message and God's power that are at our disposal even today.

When I was a child I heard preachers saying that America couldn't last two more years, or four more years, or five more years without collapsing. Let's agree to never make such predictions because we cannot presume to know God's mind. Sometimes God's patience appears endless. Aren't you glad that God has not dealt with us after our sins, nor rewarded us according to our iniquities?

So let us plead for mercy even as we know we deserve even further judgment. "Who knows? God may turn and relent" (Jonah 3:9).

ON GOD'S SIDE

1. America has received great blessings from God. Would it be accurate to say that we deserved those blessings? Why or why not? What does God's Word tell us about God's perspective on that question?

2. From the accounts of God's dealings with His people in the Old Testament, what have we learned about God's patience and mercy regarding the sins of nations?

3. For what reasons might God reverse an intended judgment? See Jeremiah 26:19. What did King Hezekiah do that caused God to reverse His impending judgment of Judah?

4. In the case of Old Testament Nineveh, and likely eighteenth-century England, repentance and faith played a part in God's withholding His judgment. What kinds of influences can the church in America provide to help halt our nation's downward spiritual spiral and reverse the trend?

WHOSE SIDE IS GOD ON?

AND NOW WE come to the heart of the matter: Does God take sides? And if so, whose side is He on . . . Is God on our side?

No nation can claim that God is on its side. We do not have a covenant with God as did ancient Israel. We cannot say that God is in our corner standing by to fight our battles and keep the American dream alive. Just as Israel erred in taking the ark of God into battle hoping that this object would win the battle for them, so we cannot take God into battle expecting Him to win on our behalf. God has certainly blessed the United States, but it would be presumption for us to think that He would "take our side" in the many struggles that we face internationally and domestically.

God is not an American. He is not Dutch or German. He is neither Republican nor Democrat. Pastor and author Kim Riddlebarger writes, "We cannot invoke him as the king and defender of our nation, although his providential purposes may indeed be to preserve us and use our nation to further his mysterious ends. To invoke God as our national defender is a especially egregious example of using God to further sinful and proud human ends."[1]

Let God Be God

The same "God is on our side mentality" has done much harm throughout the history of the church. A friend gave me a Nazi belt buckle that has the Christian cross engraved in the center. Yes, the Nazis believed very deeply that God was on their side. So did the armies of Europe when they instituted the Crusades, some of which included children who were recruited and then died by the thousands. We think of how fervently terrorists believe they are doing the will of Allah, and that he is "on their side." In Christian thought God also has been often invoked for political ends, but history shows He will not be so used.

To quote Riddlebarger again, "Instead of letting God be God, our sinful pride leads us to make such pronouncements that are not ours to make. In these cases, God is not sovereign, he is a mascot."[2] These types of "God is on our side" pronouncements demean God's reputation before the watching world. Yes, God becomes a means to our own selfish ends. History has shown that patriotism can often replace the Gospel as the chief expression of Christian commitment.

Richard Land, president of the Southern Baptists Ethics

and Liberty Commission, wrote these words in his excellent book, *The Divided States of America*, "What liberals and conservatives both are missing is that America has been blessed by God in unique ways—we are not just another country, but neither are we God's special people. I do not believe that America is God's chosen nation. God established one chosen nation and people: the Jews. We are not Israel. We do not have 'God on our side.' We are not God's gift to the world."[3]

I agree. Obviously, we do not have a covenant with God, and even if we did, we have violated our blessings in ways that are particularly heinous. Then Land continues with this important line: "America does not have a special claim on God. *Millions of Americans do, however, believe God has a special claim on them—and their country.*"[4]

Yes, and I am among those millions of Americans!

Land is right. We do not have a claim on God, but God has a claim on us. We are indeed a fortunate people, for we drink from wells we did not dig and we eat fruit from trees we did not plant. There is no doubt we will be judged nationally and individually with stricter judgment for "unto whom much is given, much is required." We've done plenty to expect judgment, not blessing.

That said, we can, however, confidently declare that God is always on the side of His people, especially when they walk in obedience and holiness. That does not mean, of course, that we as believers can expect that He will always defend us or keep us from personal tragedy. We get cancer and die in accidents, and Christian soldiers are gunned down just like everyone else.

The Christian does not put his hope in the world, because he knows that even for Jesus, this world is a dangerous place. We do, however, have the assurance of His presence in this life and the equal assurance of eternal life in the age to come.

We are not abandoned even when life caves in and the worst this world can give is thrown at us. Paul put it this way, "We are afflicted in every way, but not crushed; perplexed, but not driven to despair; persecuted, but not forsaken; struck down, but not destroyed; always carrying in the body the death of Jesus, so that the life of Jesus may also be manifested in our bodies" (2 Corinthians 4:8–11). We know that nothing can separate us from His love.

ARE WE ON GOD'S SIDE?

I marvel, as I'm sure you have, at the wisdom of Abraham Lincoln, America's most admired president. He was asked whether God was on his side and he replied, "I do not care whether God is on my side; the important question is whether I am on God's side, for God is always right." Yes, that is the important question: *Are we on God's side?*

When approaching Jericho, Joshua saw a man with a sword in his hand, "Are you for us, or for our adversaries?" he asked. This heavenly soldier answered, "No; but I am the commander of the army of the Lord" (Joshua 5:13–14). In effect God was saying, "I am not here to take sides; *I am here to take over!*"

So, the best we can do is to find out how to make sure we are on God's side. That will not guarantee that we will be spared as a nation but then again perhaps He will show us His favor. Our greatest gift to this country is to return to the biblical priorities of the church, and, more importantly, in so doing we will be pleasing to our heavenly Father.

If God does sometimes stay His severe hand of judgment, how do we readjust our agenda as a church to reflect His priorities? And how do we shift from wanting our will to be done to wanting His will? How do we get on God's side?

Preparing our hearts for what *God wants to do* rather than convincing Him to help us in what *we want to do* should be at the top of our agenda. He owes us nothing; we owe Him everything.

ON GOD'S *SIDE*

1. Can America claim confidently that God is on its side? Discuss your rationale. Within what context might any people or nation expect God's blessing?

2. Read 2 Corinthians 4:8–11. In spite of persecution, or whatever may happen in this life, what is the basis for a believer's hope? As believers, what assurances may we embrace?

3. What did Joshua discover when he confronted the heavenly soldier on the way to Jericho? (See Joshua 5:13–14.) Observe Joshua's immediate response to the

soldier's reply in Joshua 5:14. What truths might we learn from this account?

4. Whether personally or as a nation, what is the key to being on God's side?

SIDING WITH GOD
IN OUR NATIONAL LIFE

FOR A MOMENT LET ME return to some critical questions: Is the American dream and the Christian dream one and the same? If not, how are they different? If America maintains her strength and power, can we be sure that the church will be strong and powerful?

Or, is it possible for the church to remain strong even with an economic meltdown? What of "your" candidate lost the election? What if emerging world powers such as China seem to threaten America's dominance? What—if anything—does this mean for Christ's church?

When we are angry, it is possible to do the wrong thing. Our first inclination is to lash out, insisting that it is time to "take this country back." The question is how shall we as Christians influence a culture that often seems in opposition?

Let Us Showcase Christ

The Bible has the answer for us. We must return to the Gospel of our forefathers, the supernatural God of the apostles and their followers. Our responsibility in the world is to showcase Christ, to put Him on display so that the world can see what He is able to do in the lives of those who trust Him. We are to show His "worthiness" and invite others to believe in Him.

We are to represent Christ even when the society at large does not. This is not the first time that the church has had the responsibility of representing Christ when society as a whole has abandoned God. Indeed, all the churches in the New Testament were islands of righteousness in a sea of paganism. We must recapture the church as an institution for renewal rather than simply an agent for bitter confrontation. We have a hope that transcends the political landscape.

If we are to line up with God's side in our national conflict, I believe we have to return to some basic principles:

Choosing the Right Battle

First, we must *choose the right battle.*

I've already stressed that our real conflict is neither cultural, moral, or political, but doctrinal and spiritual. We can argue that Christian morality is better; we can try to clean up our culture by legislation and boycotts. But our efforts will often be like trying to mop up the floor with the faucet running. We are trying to convince citizens of earth to live as though they are citizens of heaven. And they are not buying what we are selling.

Why should we convince the unconverted to lead in a prayer in public schools? How can we expect them to pray to a God whom they neither know nor love? Our responsibility is not to put prayer back in our public schools but, as Pastor Jim Cymbala has said, to put it back in our churches and homes. Remember, God's agenda is the conversion of the heart, not merely the convincing of the mind.

The central message for us is always the lordship of Jesus and gift of salvation He came to bring us as sinners. The cross must always stand alone, unopposed by competing loyalties. Its message must never be sacrificed on the altar of our own political or social agenda, or by which political party is in office. Of course political policy has an effect on our lives, but right laws are limited in their power; they cannot make people good, nor can they make godly families. Our message must be more radical than any governmental policy could possibly be. It is a message that must penetrate the depths of the human heart.

Let us be warned. P. T. Forsythe, when speaking of the cross as the focal point of God's work for sinners, wrote, "If you move faith from that centre, you have driven the nail into the church's coffin. The church then is doomed to death, and it is only a matter of time when she shall expire."[1] The church can only live and breathe at the cross; without it there is no life and no reason to exist. Perhaps this explains why many of our churches are on life support.

We as believers should not invest our time and dollars in dispensing good advice but rather Good News. Recently I've heard it put this way: If a general wins a battle, he sends his messengers home to declare that there is good news of victory. If he loses, he sends his messengers back home to give them his best advice. As Christians we are inundated with good advice; what we need to hear again and again is good news.

The triumphant Christ is able to help us navigate the dark days ahead. We are tempted to think that our times are unique. But the fact is that the disciples and their followers had all of our national woes, times ten. They had no political base, no voting bloc in the Roman senate, and not as much as one sympathetic Roman emperor. Yet those followers of Christ changed their world, turning it "upside down," as Luke the historian put it (Acts 17:6). Certainly the advance of the American church is influenced by what happens in Washington —but it is not dependent on it. I say it again: In other eras the church has often not only survived but even grown in the face of state opposition.

We have a message that is even more important than saving America: It is holding the cross high so that God might be pleased to save Americans. We say to both Republicans and Democrats that without Jesus all of us are eternally lost.

Our first calling is to lovingly confront the greatest lie in America: that each person can come to God in his own way, with or without the sacrifice and priesthood of Jesus Christ. This is the lie that we must expose; this is the message we must embody. It is nothing less than defending the uniqueness of Christ in the face of a blizzard of religious options.

We are to defend Christ and His message winsomely, not

pushing the Gospel down people's throats but enticing them with our personal peace and respect for them as individuals. We must be known as those who love God and love the same world that He loves.

Every church in America should offer courses in basic apologetics, that is, the study of how to answer objections that unbelievers have about Christianity. Unfortunately many Christians are intimidated and thus are silenced in their witness. Have we forgotten that if there is any good news in America, it will not come from Washington, but through the lips of God's people? We cannot evangelize America unless every Christian begins to witness for Christ wherever God has planted him/her.

Somewhere I read that the loss of the Gospel in England took place during a transitional time when the Gospel was still preached, but the cross was "so bedecked with flowers that no one could see it!" What a description of our present situation. Today, the cross is covered with the "flowers" of health and wealth, the "flowers" of felt need sermonettes, and the "flowers" of political endorsements. We can add to that, the "flowers" of therapeutic techniques and entertaining worship services. And having lost the message of the cross and its implications, we have lost our greatest potential to rescue this nation.

When Paul entered the pagan city of Corinth, he didn't begin a campaign to clean up the city's morals. He preached Christ crucified, urging them to flee from the city of man to the city of God. His first duty was to cleanse the church of the sins of the culture, and then the congregation would be better prepared to spread its influence beyond its walls.

Of course, Christians should be fighting pornography, gambling, and other moral sins that plague our society. But as I've already emphasized, when we oppose such societal sins, we should appeal to common grace, and persuade others to help us in our moral crusades. But let us not think that getting a community to change its laws means that it has been "Christianized" or that its citizens are closer to believing the Gospel. Christianity, properly understood, is a message that a holy God punishes sin, and if we do not flee to the protection of Christ, we will be dammed forever. Redemption and not reformation is what we should be about.

And even as we fight societal sins, we should be working for reforms that promote justice, honor, and charity. We can and should fulfill the call of Micah to please God by seeking "to do justice, and to love kindness, and to walk humbly with [our] God" (6:8).

Simple as it sounds, we must return to the Gospel as the one integrating message for all we do and stand for. God is pleased to bless the message of the cross when it is both shared and lived.

THE WEAPON OF DEPENDENCE ON GOD

Second, *we must use the right weapons.*

Yes, dark days do lie ahead for the church. At a 2008 meeting of the National Religious Broadcasters, attendees were told that Congress was poised to pass a tidal wave of legislative and public policy decisions that make us as ministers of the Gospel open to prosecution. For example, there is "hate speech" legislation in the offing that in recent months passed both houses of Congress but was stopped on a technicality by two senators just before passage. The intention of this legislation is to silence the church on matters related to biblical sexuality. The point is this: any opposition to homosexuality can be deemed "hate speech," which means nothing less than *the criminalization of free speech.*

When an amendment was proposed that would protect churches from criminalization on the grounds of religious freedom, it was voted down. One of the senators who favors passage of this bill argued that so-called hate speech was "domestic terrorism" and must be fought with funds used to fight the terrorists.

If this legislation should pass—and it might—we can expect lawsuits against churches and those of us in the media who teach a biblical view of sexual relationships. If we want to know the consequences of such legislation, we need to remember that a pastor in Sweden, which has similar laws, was jailed for reading Romans 1 in his church, and a pastor in Canada was given three hundred hours of community service in an Islamic community center because he objected to the Quran being given out to pupils in a public school.[2]

Other possible legislation such as the so-called fairness doctrine has wide support in Congress, which would mandate that both sides of "controversial issues" have to be presented on radio and television. What is more controversial than the belief that Jesus is the only way to God? Or that homosexuality is not compatible with biblical teaching? There are other similar bills in the offing that would criminalize all public expressions of Christianity. Although we must use our constitutional rights to stand against these developments, it is clear that we might lose these battles.

Fortunately, we have powerful weapons available. Our first and foremost weapon is *helpless dependence on God's Word*. Jesus explained to His disciples that He was sending them out "like sheep among wolves." There is no hope for the survival of the sheep unless they stay close to the shepherd. There was a time when we might have thought that holy living was optional, but not in this present hour. We need godly people who love God to stand in for us with prayer and fervent intercession. God is getting our attention.

Several times I have stood in the "Luther Stube" in the Wartburg Castle where, it is said, Luther threw an inkwell at the Devil (enterprising tour leaders used to put soot on the wall so as not to disappoint tourists!). But an inkwell thrown at the Devil would hardly do the fiend harm; you cannot fight against a spirit with a material weapon!

Perhaps there is a better explanation of what happened in that room. In his Table Talks, Luther said that he "fought the devil with ink." Very probably he meant that he fought the Devil through the translation of the New Testament into German, a feat accomplished in that small room in just eleven weeks! What an inkwell could never accomplish, the Word of God did!

Let me say candidly that in many evangelical churches, the Word of God is not faithfully taught. Even among those who believe its message, there are many who choose to focus on some of the more positive aspects of Scripture, without declaring "The whole counsel of God" as the saying goes. As a result, the Gospel itself lies buried amid a host of other priorities and so-called "practical" matters. Meanwhile, all of our efforts of marketing techniques, pandering to felt needs, and preaching a gospel of human potential are as effective as throwing inkwells at the Devil! Sadly, *we might not even know that we have embraced the gods of modernity.*

We can no longer assume that we will have a president or a congress that sympathizes with goals of the Christian faith. We have to get used to the reality that many in our government see us as an enemy that must be silenced and whose influence must be marginalized. What do we do when Congress enacts legislation that would, in effect, criminalize Gospel preaching? What can we do if hate crime legislation produces lawsuits that cripple our Christian ministries on radio and television? We will only be discouraged if we focus on our newspapers more than we do our Bibles.

Our hope in a better world enables us to be optimistic in this confused age in which we are called to represent our triumphant Lord. We are convinced that God is in charge of what happens in His world. Indeed, we remember that not even the wicked can exist without God's express permission and power. Like the early Christians, we should give thanks that we were found worthy to suffer for His name (see Philippians 1:29). Paul did not view his imprisonment as a hindrance to the Gospel but, in some sense, as actully furthering it! (Philippians 1:12–14).

We have the responsibility of educating our congregations

on what is happening in Washington and in the wider culture. We should become informed about the position of various candidates on the issues that are important to us and vote accordingly. And yet, while we work to better the outcome of elections, we must never lose focus on the underlying spiritual battles that even more directly affect the moral and spiritual climate of our nation. Let us humbly admit that we have slid too far to think that we can reverse the course of this nation simply by having "the right people" in Washington. The unseen battle is even more fierce than the one we see in our newspapers and on television.

Even now in this critical hour, I wonder if God has our attention. Are we ready to cry to Him in helpless repentance? Are we ready to test God's promises against the backdrop of moral and spiritual confusion? Can we trust God when our cultural props are kicked from under us?

THE WEAPON OF OUR LIFESTYLE

If our first weapon is a renewed dependence on God's Word, our second weapon is the integrity of our lifestyle. Put simply, *if we want to reach our culture, we must suffer well.*

In the future, we can expect that the target of many of the attacks will be *The Name.* After Peter and John spent a night in prison, their angry critics agreed to "warn them to speak no more to anyone in *this name*" (Acts 4:17, italics added). But Peter and John famously replied, "Whether it is right in the sight of God to listen to you rather than to God, you must judge, for we cannot but speak of what we have seen and heard" (verses 19– 20).

I confess that we as a church, pampered as we are, are woefully unprepared for blatant persecution. But history shows that persecution produces a certain kind of Christian, the kind that we've not see too often in our beloved country.

Peter explains what our response should be:

> Beloved, do not be surprised at the fiery trial when it comes upon you to test you, as though something strange were happening to you. But rejoice insofar as you share Christ's sufferings, that you may also rejoice and be glad when his glory is revealed. If you are insulted for the name of Christ, you are blessed, because the Spirit of glory and of God rests upon you. But let none of you suffer as a murderer or a thief or an evildoer or as a meddler. Yet if anyone suffers as a Christian, let him not be ashamed, but let him glorify God in that name. (1 Peter 4:12–16)

Dietrich Bonhoeffer said accurately, "Suffering is not an interruption, but our calling." Paul wrote that we are to share in the sufferings of Christ. This is the pain we endure because of Christ; the choices we make because He is our example. In our suffering we conform to the likeness of Christ. Let me repeat: He *calls* us to suffer. That is a crucial part of the Christian lifestyle. There is joy in Jesus, yes. There is also suffering for His name.

ARE WE READY?

As our culture drifts into paganism, we as Christians *fear* the suffering that might come our way. Employees fear that they might not be able to witness for Christ, given new laws that declare that workplaces are "religion free." Parents are increasingly isolated from the school systems that promote homosexual lifestyles, sexual freedom, and radical individualism. Churches fear they will lose their tax-exempt status if they do not marry homosexual couples.

Such suffering—indeed, *any* suffering for Christ in our culture—is largely unknown to us. But other countries have not been exempt; in fact, more people are dying for their faith in the face of hostile cultures and political regimes than at any time in history. Perhaps our time will come. We should not fear suffering for the name of Christ.

To quote Bonhoeffer once more, "Where the world exploits [the Christian] will dispossess himself, and where the world oppresses, he will stoop down and raise up the oppressed. If the world refuses justice, the Christian will pursue mercy, and if the world takes refuge in lies, he will open his mouth for the dumb, and bear testimony to the truth . . . for Jew or Greek, bond or free, strong or weak, noble or base."[3]

Michael Baumgarten, a nineteenth-century Lutheran pastor who was excommunicated because of his adherence to a true Gospel, wrote, "There are times in which lectures and publications no longer suffice to communicate the necessary truth. At such times the deeds and sufferings of the saints must create a new alphabet in order to reveal again the secret of truth."[4] Suffering communicates the Gospel in a new language; it authenticates the syllables that flow so easily from our lips. When the chaff is separated from the wheat, the kernels germinate and grow. *It is not how loud we can shout but how well we can suffer that will convince the world of the integrity of our message.*

There is a story about a pilgrim making his way to the Promised Land. He was carrying his master's cross, a burden he cheerfully accepted. Though he did notice that the farther he walked, the heavier it became. But as the pilgrim became weary, he sat down to rest and noticed a woodsman nearby. "Good friend," the pilgrim called, "could I use your axe to shorten my cross?" The woodsman complied.

The pilgrim traveled on, making much progress. He was glad, for the cross was shorter, his burden lighter. He continued his pilgrimage but then suddenly came to a deep gulf that separated him from the next steps en route to the Promised Land. He could see that he could use the cross as a bridge to span the divide. But alas, it fell short by the very length he had cut off.

Just then the pilgrim awoke; it was only a dream. And now with tears streaming down his face, he clutched his cross to his breast, and pressed on. The cross was just as heavy, but its burden was lighter.

There are many things we can do to counter efforts to silence the Gospel. We can organize politically, we can angrily denounce our enemies, or we can prudently choose to carry our cross, *all of it*. The pilgrim offers us a lesson here: *The lighter our cross, the weaker our witness.*

We must bring the cross out of our churches and carry it to a hurting world. Our task is not to save America but to save Americans by living the Gospel. "Keep your behavior excellent among the Gentiles, so that in the thing in which they slander you as evildoers, they may because of your good deeds, as they observe them, glorify God in the day of visitation" (1 Peter 2:12 NASB).

The average person will never be convinced of the credibility of the cross until he becomes personally acquainted with someone who lives out the Christian faith, applying its implications to every situation, even at great personal cost.

Many Americans have never met someone who is pro-life toward the unborn child, yet also loves women who have had abortions. Many believe they have never met anyone who is opposed to the homosexual agenda, yet loves homosexuals. They do not know someone who is opposed to sex education and yet is willing to work with the school board to find an alternative. I believe that there are tens of thousands of Christians who have been reduced to silence by the loud din of the media as it smothers us with pro-abortion, pro-homosexual rhetoric.

Let no one say that I advocate withdrawing from our cultural and spiritual battles. I am simply saying we must fight with different weapons. I've emphasized that our greatest weapon is not politics, important though that is, but the blessed news of the Gospel, faithfully lived and proclaimed. And if we can see suffering as our calling, our lifestyles can show the credibility of our message. There are some things only God's Word faithfully believed and lived can do.

There is a final weapon in our battle to rightly represent God's side. The weapon goes right to the heart of the matter, as we will see.

ON GOD'S *SIDE*

1. To line up with God's side in our national conflict, we first must choose the right battle. Given the immense challenges facing the church in America, what is the "right battle"? Why is it the supreme battle?

2. Discuss the intentions of "hate speech" and "fairness doctrine" legislation. What might be the outcome if the church loses those battles? What can we do as individuals to preserve the freedoms we currently enjoy?

3. Read Matthew 10:15–17, the passage in which Jesus tells His disciples that He is "sending them out like sheep among wolves." How relevant is that statement for today's church? What advice did Jesus give His disciples in this passage? What encouragements may we draw from knowing that Jesus is also our Shepherd?

4. Dr. Lutzer also points out that we must use the right weapons—the first being our dependence on God's Word. How can our dependence on and use of the full counsel of God's Word give us a powerful advantage?

5. There is another effective weapon—the integrity of our lifestyle. Discuss 1 Peter 2:12 and 4:12–16. How does the suffering of believers become an effective weapon in reaching our culture?

WINNING EVEN
WHEN WE LOSE

EVERY SOLDIER needs to have the proper weapons for success in battle. But the right weapons alone don't assure victory. Deep down, the troops must believe they can win. They trust their command; they follow their commander, who gives them courage and passion. If they believe what he says, they have faith they can succeed.

This is an issue of the heart. When we follow Christ, we must imitate Him, showing the same compassion, mercy, and respect He showed for all who were living away from God, some ignorantly and some defiantly. Either way, Jesus loved them. Likewise, we must *fight with the right attitude*. That is our final weapon to succeed in drawing a nation back to God—a humble heart filled with compassion and mercy.

Yes, we must speak up bravely in behalf of preborn infants. Yes, we need to point toward bringing an end to racism and passing just laws. But we fight with meekness—with an attitude of humility. We do not approach society as if we have all the answers for the escalation of violence and child abuse. We do not pretend that if we were in charge, our moral toboggan slide would end.

GIVING OUR REASONS WITH
GENTLENESS AND RESPECT

The apostle Peter wrote that we should give a reason for our hope "with gentleness and respect, having a good conscience, so that, when you are slandered, those who revile your good behavior in Christ may be put to shame. For it is better to suffer for doing good if that should be God's will, than for doing evil" (1 Peter 3:16–17).

"Even mercy without tears is self-righteousness," says Bible teacher Steve Brown. We engage society, not to lord it over others, nor to self-righteously point out their sins. We serve, knowing that the sins that exist in the world are also found in the church. We have no illusions that the city of man (the world) can become sanctified. We pray for our country as Abraham did for Sodom and Gomorrah, knowing that we have relatives who live within its gates. We are also the first to help the single mother who does not know how she can cope with her baby. We reach out to those who have AIDS, not with self-righteous condemnation, but with the recognition that we too could easily fall victim to this disease. We always judge ourselves more harshly than we judge others.

How do we connect with those who hate us? Jim Garlow, pastor of Skyline Church in San Diego, California, challenged me by telling about the evolution of his thinking about his relationship with those who perceive us to be their enemies. He felt guilty because of the conflict he had had with a man he had helped vote off the school board; he felt guilty because he had never made contact with a lesbian pastor and other homosexuals in the area. So he met with a few of these people and asked them to educate him on how they could be friends even though they could never possibly agree on the issues that divided them. He discovered that friendships can be formed even with those who see us as their natural enemies. Minds were not changed but attitudes have been. To reach out over troubled waters with such humility, in my opinion, makes Jesus "look good."

When a member of Congress is sworn in with his hand on the Quran rather than the Bible, we grieve for the direction that our nation is going. But we do not organize protests; we do not denounce him angrily as he walks up the Capitol steps. We realize that as our nation becomes more pluralistic we must give other people the same respect as we would like to be given. The same freedom of speech that we insist on for ourselves we give to Jews, Muslims, and the secularists. We believe in a "civil public square" where various ideas can be debated but with respect for all, despite race and religion.

We do not take the cross that should humble us and turn it into a club that would make the world "shape up." We pursue our primary mission with single-mindedness and heartfelt conviction. We are convinced that America cannot be restored by a change of administrations in Washington, even if we had a "Christian" party.

What do you do if your children are expected to see steamy sex films in schools as a part of the sex education curriculum? You go to the teacher and try to resolve the matter. If that doesn't work, you go to the school board and if necessary join a coalition of parents who are willing to protest this violation of parent/child responsibility. You do not antagonize others by strong words of condemnation, or by demonizing those who don't see matters your way. You realize that by your life and attitude Christ is on display.

Eventually you might realize, as millions have, that your children have to be withdrawn from the school system to be taught at home either by you or by other families working together. Incredibly, we have to learn lessons of survival from our brothers and sisters who lived in the Soviet Union during the many years when their children had to be sent to government schools for indoctrination.

What do pastors do when they are told that their church will lose its tax-exempt status if they refuse to marry homosexual couples? Ministers can seek to block that legislation, arguing that the churches and other charitable organizations provide valuable services to the community. But neither pastors nor church members call their opponents names but hope that reason will prevail. Let us seek the involvement of legal experts, but let us not imply that the church that is built upon Christ will whither away if tax exemption were denied.

We must disagree wisely. Our speech is always to be "seasoned with salt." If a child is forbidden to draw a Nativity scene in school, we talk to the teacher, to school administrators. We try to work with those who belong to the city of man, rather than generating needless antagonism.

We must disagree honestly. We must never misrepresent our adversaries in an appeal letter to our constituency so that we might generate anger that in turn generates money. Unfortunately, we all receive fund-raising appeals that are sensational, overblown, and intended to make us angry (conventional wisdom says that only angry people send money). Equally foolish is the assumption that the organization that wants our funds is actually in a position to fix whatever has gone wrong!

We disagree humbly. We don't complain when the media is unfair just as Christ didn't complain when the soldiers were unfair. We don't castigate others as if our cause is dependent on endorsements or "fair reporting." Have we who are on the other side of this volatile issue always been "fair"? Since many of our Christians often don't act "Christianly," why should we expect such behavior from the unconverted? We should not be alarmed if unbelievers act like unbelievers; we should be alarmed, however, when believers act like *un*believers!

We should not only believe in racial reconciliation but model it. We should stand up for the rights of the poor, the marginalized, and the outcasts. We are haunted by Bonhoeffer's famous question based on Matthew 25:35–40, "Who is Jesus Christ for us? You will recall that Jesus said that when we feed his people, *we feed him*; when we visit his people in prison, *we visit him*; when we clothe his people, *we clothe him*. So who is Jesus Christ for you? And for me? *If only we could see that it is Jesus Christ who suffers among us.*"

A Love That Defies Explanation

Bishop Samuel, who died in a hail of gunfire with President Anwar Sadat of Egypt back in 1981, once told Dr. Ray Bakke how Christianity captured northern Africa in the early centuries. He spoke about the love of the Christians that defied explanation. For example, in those days there were no abortion procedures, so unwanted children were just left to die on the streets. So there would be "baby runs" with young men rescuing abandoned infants. This was, of course, before baby bottles, so the infants were brought to nursing mothers who adopted them as their own.

Samuel, leader of Egypt's Christian Coptic Church, described how Christians were often discriminated against and given lowly positions such as garbage collectors. Yet when these lowly Christians came across dead bodies (often as the result of a plague), they would wash the bodies and give them a decent burial, arguing that even the wicked deserve a burial in light of the coming resurrection. Such acts of love stimulated the interest of the pagans: They were impressed by a supernatural love, a love of service even to the people of the world. And with their hearts, these Christians won North Africa to the Christian faith.

We should not see ourselves as the "persecuted minority" whining about how difficult the world has made it for us. We humbly acknowledge that unless God helps us we will not be helped; unless we are redeemed in His grace, we shall be lost. We stand with sinners, acknowledging that apart from unmerited grace, we would be where they are today. We do what is right and take the consequences. And if we have to go to jail, we rejoice that we were "counted worthy to suffer shame for His name" (Acts 5:41 NKJV).

Meanwhile, we have work to do. We have to intentionally rectify our reputation, which has been tarnished by the well-meaning radicals among us. We can only win America if every single Christian becomes an activist, assuming the delicate task of taking a firm and loving stand on the issues, yet presenting spiritual healing to a society that is afflicted with the disease called sin. We are to hold up the cross and display "the excellencies of Him who has called [us] out of darkness into His marvelous light" (1 Peter 2:9 NASB).

We must learn, as have our brothers and sisters who have suffered for His name, that *it is not necessary for us to win in this world in order to win in the next.*

HOPE FOR THE HEART!

History has shown and the Bible confirms that *it is possible for the kingdom of man to decline and the kingdom of God to survive and even grow*! In fact, the church has the responsibility of picking up the pieces of a rotting society. As Augustine would put it, the city of God does not depend upon the city of man for its existence and strength. Today as everything that has ever been nailed down is torn up, we have the privilege of coming in the name of Christ to people in need.

Missionary experts tell us that the church in mainland China, where vicious persecution has been felt for the past fifty years, has grown more than the church in Taiwan with its freedoms. I say this not to glorify persecution, since I for one would not take kindly to imprisonment; I would find it hard to be joyful if we had to shut down our media ministry because the Federal Communications Commission has made regulations that strangle our ministry. But I say such painful setbacks may actually contribute to the success of the city of God, for God's success does not depend on the favor of the city of man. We are, after all, pilgrims en route to our permanent home, and *nothing—including persecution and even death—can stop God's cause in the world.*

I pray for and support all Christian legal organizations that continue to fight for freedom of speech for ourselves and others. I'm glad that we have those nonpartisan ministries who keep us up-to-date on what is happening in Washington and urge us to keep our constituencies informed as to what Congress and the president are up to. However, even such freedom can be an idol. Read the history of the church in Europe, Russia, and China and you will be convinced that *it is not necessary to have freedom in order to be faithful.*

The bottom line is that *we must seek God.* More than electing the right president, we need to have the right heart before God—this year and every year before Jesus returns. I believe very deeply that only God can save us from the night that is engulfing us. Of course, we have always believed that only God can preserve our freedoms and turn our nation back from its rush to ruin. But never have we needed His intervention so desperately; never before have we felt so helpless in the face of massive political and moral movements that we cannot stop.

Ours is a battle that cannot be won just by reason, scientific data, and dialogue.

And if we keep in mind that prayer, as Henry Blackaby says, is not to convince God to do what we want, but "for us to get in line with what he wants to do," then we will pray with faith and anticipation. We will not only pray that this nation be delivered from its woes but that we will be faithful regardless of whether we see our battles won or not.

One day the king Jehosaphat woke up and was told that a vast army was coming against him. The king asked God what to do, so he proclaimed a fast throughout the land of Judah. The people then gathered from every town in the land to seek help from the Lord. Jehoshaphat then stood in the temple of the Lord, and prayed.

> O Lord, God of our fathers, are you not the God who is in heaven? You rule over all the kingdoms of the nations. Power and might are in your hand, and no one can withstand you. O our God, did you not drive out the inhabitants of this land before your people Israel and give it forever to the descendants of Abraham your friend? . . . "If calamity comes upon us, whether the sword of judgment, or plague or famine, we will stand in your presence before this temple that bears your Name and will cry out to you in our distress, and you will hear us and save us." . . . O our God, will you not judge them [the adversaries]? *For we have no power to face this vast army that is attacking us. We do not know what to do, but our eyes are upon you.* (2 Chronicles 20: 6–9, 12 NIV, italics added)

"We do not know what to do, but our eyes are upon you," King Jehosaphat said. I wonder what would happen if millions of believers set aside their schedules to seek God on behalf of this nation, as Jehosaphat and his people did. What would happen if privately and corporately, we confessed our sins and turned away from our own idols? Perhaps God would intervene so the destruction of marriage and the forces that seek to tear our families apart would be stayed.

After Jehosaphat has prayed, the word of the Lord came through a man anointed with the Spirit: "Do not be afraid or discouraged because of this vast army. For the battle is not yours but God's" (verse 15 NIV). Then the king commanded that a select group of men walk ahead of the army singing and praising God for the splendor of His holiness.

And God gave the victory!

Please understand that God does not owe us such a deliverance. No nation has turned away so much light in order to choose darkness. No nation has squandered as many opportunities as we have. We can only call on God for mercy, and if it please Him, He will come to our aid. We certainly cannot expect a revival simply because we do not want to face the harassment that well might come to us all. But if we humble ourselves, weeping for this nation, God may yet intervene and restore decency to this crazed world. Most of all, we should pray that millions would be converted and belong to God forever. We are in God's hands, knowing that people change their minds only when God changes their hearts.

If we cannot weep before God, we are probably not fit to declare the truth before men. Let us submit to God's will for us and for our nation.

Only He can save us now. And if He doesn't, we will still worship and serve Him with joy.

ON GOD'S SIDE

1. Read 1 Peter 3: 16–17. The final weapon in the church's battle to succeed is the right attitude. Why is this weapon effective in engaging our society?

2. Our Christian beliefs and convictions will be challenged. As we realize that we display Christ by our lives and attitudes, how should that temper our approach toward those who disagree with us? Discuss the benefits of disagreeing wisely, honestly, and humbly with others, even those who attack our faith.

3. Dr. Lutzer points out that it is not necessary to have freedom in order to be faithful. In parts of the world where Christians are persecuted, and even martyred, the church of Jesus Christ flourishes. What does this tell us about the dynamics of the church and the powerful spiritual resources God has given us?

4. For a church that desires revival and repentance in America, what is our most important bottom line action?

5. Read the account of King Jehosaphat in 2 Chronicles 20:6–9, 12. Can we expect that God would answer our prayers for deliverance and intervention as He did for King Jehosaphat? How seriously do you believe the church in America is currently seeking revival?

NOTES

Chapter 1: THE FIRST PRINCIPLE

1. R. C. Sproul, *When Worlds Collide* (Wheaton: Crossway, 2002), 63.

2. The American presidents typically have ended their annual report to Congress by saying, "God bless America"; sometimes by saying, "God bless this great nation," "God bless the United States," and, once, "God bless our beloved country." See http://www.thisnation.com/library/sotu/index.html.

3. Sproul, *When Worlds Collide*, 29–30.

Chapter 2: THE SECOND PRINCIPLE

1. www.news.harvard.edu/guide/intro/index.html1. Founded with a cash gift by minister John Harvard with a distinctly Christian focus whose earliest graduates included many future Puritan ministers, the college concentrations today include studies of women, gender, and sexuality (WGS), with one WGS focus in "lesbian/gay and bisexual studies" and another in "queer and feminist theory"; see http://www.fas.harvard.edu/~wgs/about/about.htm.

2. George M. Marsden, *The Soul of the American University* (New York: Oxford Univ. Press, 1994). The book's back cover copy chronicles the decline: "Only a century ago, almost all state universities held compulsory chapel services . . . Today, however, the once pervasive influence of religion in the intellectual and cultural life of America's preeminent colleges and universities has all but vanished."

3. R. C. Sproul, *When Worlds Collide* (Wheaton: Crossway, 2002), 44.

4. Lisa Beamer spoke to the nation's press as well as to television audiences on *The Oprah Winfrey Show* and *Larry King Live*. She told King she was sustained by "faith in a God who we know loves us and a God who we know is in charge of our lives and in charge of the course of events in history"; *CNN Larry King Live*, broadcast August 23, 2002. See http://www.transcripts.cnn.com/TRANSCRIPTS/0208/23/lkl.00.html.

Chapter 3. THE THIRD PRINCIPLE

1. In September 2004 adjunct professor Thomas Klocek of DePaul University challenged the views of Muslim students during a student activities fair held in a campus cafeteria. Their subsequent complaint to the administration led to Klocek meeting briefly with the college dean. Subsequently the dean notified Klocek of his suspension and, later, the decision to not renew his contract. Klocek had "demanded a hearing [over the suspension, but] his efforts proved fruitless." See http://en.wikipedia.org/wiki/Thomas_E._Klocek.

Chapter 4. THE FOURTH PRINCIPLE

1. Hurricane Katrina made landfall on August 29, 2005, as the third strongest hurricane to hit the United States and claimed more than 1,800 lives in three states along the Gulf Coast; see http://en.wikipedia.org/wiki/HurricaneKatrina. This decade's Indian Ocean tsunami (December 26, 2004) has been called "the most devastating tsunami in recorded history" by the National Institute of Oceanography, with the dead and missing estimated at more than 216,000 in eleven countries; see www.nio.org/jsp/tsunami.jsp and www.msnbc.msn.com/id/6754820.

2. See www.sharefest.com/html/about/history.asp. The first ShareFest began in central Arkansas in 1999, and today the annual event involves local churches in at least fourteen states.

Chapter 6. THE SIXTH PRINCIPLE

1. As quoted by Edward Dobson, "Taking Politics Out of the Sanctuary," *Liberty*, January/February 1997, 11.

2. As quoted in *World* magazine, August 18, 1998, 20.

3. Quoted in Cal Thomas, "Christian Coalition Has Strayed Too Far from Its True Calling," Los Angeles Times Syndicate, 1997.

4. "An Evangelical Manifesto: The Washington Declaration of Evangelical Identity and Public Commitment," Copyright © 2008, by the Evangelical Manifesto Steering Committee, 15.

5. Ibid.

6. Dobson, "Taking Politics Out of the Sanctuary," 11.

Chapter 8. WHOSE SIDE IS GOD ON?

1. Kim Riddlebarger, "Using God," *Modern Reformation*, November/December 2007, 14.

2. Ibid.

3. Richard Land, *The Divided States of America* (Nashville: Nelson, 2007), 192.

4. Ibid, emphasis added.

Chapter 9. SIDING WITH GOD IN OUR NATIONAL LIFE

1. As quoted in John Stott, *The Cross of Christ* (Downers Grove, Ill.: Inter-Varsity, 1986), 44.

2. Janet L. Folger, *The Criminalization of Christianity* (Sisters, Oreg.: Multnomah, 2005), 28–29. This remarkable book details the agenda and techniques of radical liberals who are determined to make it a crime for Christians to practice their faith.

3. As quoted in Eberhard Bethge, *Bonhoeffer: Exile and Martyr* (New York: Seabury, 1975), 155.

4. Ibid.

OPRAH, MIRACLES, AND THE NEW EARTH

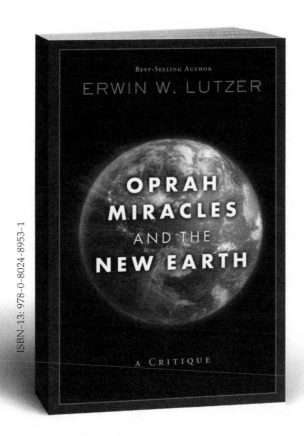

ISBN-13: 978-0-8024-8953-1

When the world's most powerful celebrity (according to *Forbes* magazine) sponsors a course on miracles, millions will join her class —including believers of every kind. With characteristic insight and clarity, Dr. Erwin W. Lutzer reveals the true nature of contemporary spirituality, tracing its roots across a range of false belief systems and back to its first appearance in the garden of Eden.

1-800-678-8812 · MOODYPUBLISHERS.COM

THE TRUTH ABOUT
SAME-SEX MARRIAGE

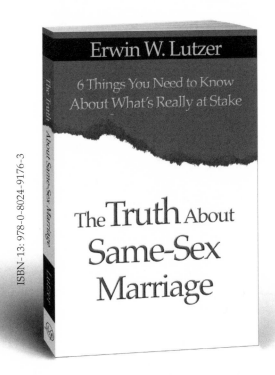

Dr. Erwin W. Lutzer, pastor of the Moody Church in Chicago and esteemed theologian, responds to the attacks that marriage has sustained over the past several years. His answers will help you formulate your own answers to outspoken opponents of the biblical definition of marriage.

MOODY
PUBLISHERS.

1-800-678-8812 · MOODYPUBLISHERS.COM